BYRTHRITE

'Sarah Daniels' welcome new play takes a backward glance to the 17th century to pinpoint the moment when control over women's bodies passed into the hands of men . . . both a rattling good yarn . . . and a Cassandra-like warning of the dangers in our own time that we would do well to heed . . . *Byrthrite* proves that Sarah Daniels is a writer at the peak of her power'

Lyn Gardner, *City Limits*

'Daniels puts her case with vigour and wit'

Claire Armistead, *Financial Times*

SARAH DANIELS' plays include *Ripen Our Darkness* (Royal Court Theatre Upstairs, London, 1981); *Ma's Flesh Is Grass* (Crucible Studio Theatre, Sheffield, 1981); *Penumbra* (Sheffield University Theatre, 1981); *The Devil's Gateway* (Royal Court Theatre Upstairs, London, 1983), *Masterpieces* (Manchester Royal Exchange, 1983; Royal Court Theatre, London 1983/4) and *Neaptide,* winner of the 1982 George Devine Award (Cottesloe, National Theatre, London, 1986). Sarah Daniels was Writer in Residence at the Royal Court Theatre in 1984.

The cover illustration is by Iain Lanyon.

by the same author

MASTERPIECES
RIPEN OUR DARKNESS & THE DEVIL'S GATEWAY
NEAPTIDE

BYRTHRITE

SARAH DANIELS

A Methuen Paperback

A METHUEN THEATRESCRIPT

First published as a paperback original in 1987
in Great Britain by Methuen London Ltd,
11 New Fetter Lane, London EC4P 4EE
and in the United States of America by
Methuen Inc, 29 West 35th Street,
New York, NY 10001

Copyright © 1987 by Sarah Daniels
Music copyright © 1987 by Jo-Anne Fraser

British Library Cataloguing in Publication Data
Daniels, Sarah
   Byrthrite.— (Methuen's new theatrescripts)
   I. Title
   822′.914   PR6054.A52
   ISBN 0-413-15900-0

Set in 10 point IBM Press Roman by 🅰\ Tek Art Ltd, Croydon, Surrey
Printed in Great Britain by Richard Clay Ltd, Bungay, Suffolk

Foreword

Byrthrite is set in the seventeenth century, the time when control over women's reproductive processes began to change hands from women to men. The changeover began with the introduction of new technology by male doctors, the use of forceps in childbirth. The process continued, and gathered momentum, over the following three centuries through the progressive introduction of technological interventions derived from a science and medicine organised to exclude women from significant positions within it. The organisation and development of medicine, particularly obstetrics and gynaecology, and science, particularly human genetics, is fundamental to the situation we find ourselves in today.

Reproductive technology has been defined as:

> 'Covering anything to do with the manipulation of the gametes (eggs or sperm) or the foetus, for whatever purpose from conception other than by sexual union, to treatment of disease *in utero,* to the ultimate manufacture of a human being to exact specification . . . Thus the earliest procedure . . . is artificial insemination; next . . . artificial fertilisation . . . next artificial implantation . . . in the future total extracorporal gestation . . . and finally what is popularly meant by (reproductive) engineering, the production – or better, the biological manufacture of a human being to desired specification.'

This definition, taken from the Journal of the American Medical Association was published in 1972 when the only technique that could be used to alter conception and result in a live birth was artificial insemination. Artificial fertilisation and artificial implantation resulting in a live birth did not take place until 1978 when Louise Brown was born in England, the first so-called test tube baby.

In 1986 we have three of these five processes. Total extracorporal gestation, the so-called artificial womb, followed by the biological manufacture of human beings to desired specification, of course, remain to be achieved. The development of these processes depend upon each other. The definition gives us the cumulative technological steps that need to be taken in order to gain total control over human reproduction. It also exposed the long term planning and major resource allocation needed to achieve these ends.

The new reproductive technologies are one aspect of biotechnological developments that will affect every aspect of life from the growth of food to warfare. The qualities inherent in biotechnology are those of efficiency, speed and control. In human reproduction research women, our bodies ourselves, are the experimental material.

Amid the eugenic presentation of the new reproduction technologies by the mass media, 'perfect babies for perfect couples', lies the Governmental, and ethical discussion generally. This proceeds without reference to women. The influential British Government Report of the Committee of Inquiry into Human Fertilisation and Embryology (the Warnock Report) uses a scientific, knowledge-based way of discussing reproduction. They showed no understanding that they were discussing woman's life processes. In this, and the other reports around the world based on it, women are reduced to body parts: wombs, ovaries, and fallopian tubes or subsumed within 'the couple' or 'the family', which of course is always heterosexual. Women have no existence except as biology or in relation to men.

The use of medicine and science controlled by men to challenge the independence and subjectivity of women continues as does the challenge to it by women. The prize is total control over women's reproductive processes and the reproduction of future generations. Women may at last become the vessel, the carrier, if used at all, for the male creation. In *Byrthrite* we return to the origins of this struggle.

> 'We are living in an age where technology is outstripping science fiction in its possibilities and in its language of myth and symbol and where, in the world of reproductive research, the whole idea of fathering is undergoing a profound shift of meaning. It is still a culture whose most persistent myth is that of ultimate male procreativity in the shape of God who both created the world and fathered his son through remote implantation using the medium of woman. Scientists do not have to be mad to be informed by the prevailing mythology. The technology, given the system of ideas that underlies it, is self generating, and generating new technologies at an extraordinary rate'.
>
> (Claire McDonald, Letter, *Women's Review, No. 4,* 1985).

Jalna Hanmer
University of Bradford, 1987

Byrthrite was first presented at the Royal Court Theatre Upstairs on 21 November 1986, with the following cast:

ROSE, *17*	Eleanor David
GRACE, *70*/BRIDGET, *19*	Maggie McCarthy
HELEN, *33*/ANN, *30*/PRICKER'S MOTHER, *55*	Holly Wilson
URSULA, *13*/MARY, *18*	Meera Syal
JANE, *20*/LADY H, *30*/URSULA'S MOTHER	Janette Legge
A MAN, *various ages*	David Bamber

The action takes place in the seventeenth century in the county of Essex, during the Civil War.

Part One

Scene One: The lying-in
Scene Two: Outside
Scene Three: The meeting room
Scene Four: Grace's home

Scene Five: The pond
Scene Six: Outside
Scene Seven: The servants' attic
Scene Eight: The meeting room

Part Two (two years later)

Scene One: Outside
Scene Two: The church
Scene Three: A rowing boat
Scene Four: The pond
Scene Five: The gaol

Scene Six: Grace's home
Scene Seven: The inn
Scene Eight: Grace's home
Scene Nine: The pond
Scene Ten: Grace's garden

Directed by Carole Hayman
Designed by Jenny Tiramani
Music by Jo-Anne Fraser

PART ONE

Scene One

The lying-in.
Night. ROSE *and* HELEN *outside a house.* ROSE *has almost completed carving a wooden toy and* HELEN *is finishing a baby's garment. Presently* GRACE, *a midwife, comes out to them.*

GRACE. It be a girl.

Women's voices can be heard singing from inside the house.
GRACE, ROSE *and* HELEN *join in the song.*

ALL:

The Birthing Song

Unto you a child is born
Unto you a daughter given
From this time forth go and to all
  women tell;
That the daughter's inheritance shall
  pass
Through you all, to be kept forever
Women's rite, women's right for
  choice in birth.

HELEN: How is Ann?

GRACE: In best of spirits. Mary is with her.

ROSE: And is her mind made up to a name?

GRACE: Aye, Marion. Ah there you be, Rose, now be sure and let all the women know of our plans afore this night's celebrations adle their memories.

ROSE: I'll need you to lend weight to arguments.

GRACE: By and by.

ROSE *goes inside.*

HELEN: Grace, you'll not take umbrage if I avoid the revellin'?

GRACE: Even the most rigid men allow our sex attendance at lying-in.

HELEN: Is not that.

GRACE: Aye. I know too well who I shall find outside: Rose and thyself

with not a word passed between you, no doubt.

HELEN: For our reasons could not be more contrary.

GRACE: Cam, I will walk with you.

HELEN (*shakes her head*): Let me be alone.

GRACE: I shall see you at the meeting?

HELEN: Aye. So thou shalt.

Scene Two

The meeting room.
A bare room. MARY *stands in the middle,* HELEN *at the side, watching her.* ROSE, *at the other end, her back to both of them, staring out of the window.*

MARY: I'll not stand here waiting for moon to turn to cheese.

HELEN: Is you to begin, Mary. Rose and I follow on.

MARY: Mind, if she doth 'Grace' us with an appearance I'll not start over.

HELEN: Will do harm to none of us to have our memories freshened.

MARY (*sighs, takes a deep breath and starts*): 'Verily, we enquire of the cunning woman, wilt thou pass on the knowledge of the longevity of life, and she does thus reply' (*Trying to remember the next line.*) 'and she does thus reply,' yes? (*But she can't.*) Oh, a pox on this. (*So she ad libs:*) 'And she does thus reply.' (*Very fast:*) 'I vouchsafe to thee daughter tis not so much the abominable odious persistent attention of such lewde and filthye offenders as mankynde. Tis not ...'

HELEN: Recoil thy tongue before it runs us to the rope. Do you want us hung?

MARY (*to* HELEN): Nay, those are not the lines either — still sounds good, specially as it rhymes.

HELEN: Is not for saying out loud and neither is what you just spake.

MARY: What I supposed to have said floated clean out of my skull and them others floated in.

HELEN: Well, they aren't for floating out of your mouth.

MARY: Who pray will be bowing over to correct us? At this pace not even Holy Ghost. (*Sullenly*:) Oh, what matter is it to anyone, any matter.

HELEN (*wearily*): Don't beset us with that all over.

MARY: You liked my words well enough didn't ye, Rose? (*Pause.*) Rose?

ROSE (*still with her back to them*): I can't keep watch and sort out quarrels.

MARY (*mumbles*): Plain folly.

ROSE (*turns round*): Let her say what she wants, Helen, we've not got time to be worrying over a few words.

HELEN: Let's start up one more time. Mary? I was out of course to reprimand you.

MARY: The mood has mislaid me.

HELEN (*snaps*): Seems like you had a big dump on you afore you cam.

MARY (*mutters*): Waste of precious female breath.

ROSE: Mary! How can you turn your mind round so?

MARY (*wearily*): In the first instance, singing, dancing, players, enjoyment of any kind is going against the law. (*Becoming angry.*) Second, women are never heard of doing it. And third, (*Shouts*:) one of our dramatis personae is missing!

HELEN: Keep your mouth level. Do you want for the pricker to have his irons clapped on us?

MARY: Us! Us! Us! It's always us! Not a woman in the county not lying quaking tonight a-worrying at being swam and who's doing anything 'bout it — us! Always the same.

HELEN: We should be thanking luck we don't live such a distance from each other. No place else in this country could you find handful of women with no children.

MARY (*holding up three fingers in disbelief*): This many? This many of us? I'll not swallow nature having so few singularities.

ROSE: And Grace. That's one more.

MARY (*exasperated*): And where is Grace? Where be she then?

HELEN (*with concern*): T'is unlike her not to cam at all. And there's no woman due.

MARY: Huh, the day that will be. (*Then*:) Oh Helen, forgive me, I was not thinking.

ROSE: Probably her cock got loose again. (*They laugh,* ROSE *turns back to the window.*) He's almost upon us. You and your fooling.

HELEN (*panicking*): Quick, quickly. Make haste. The psalms.

They all kneel.

MARY (*mutters*): If I try and sing a psalm in this humour it will all but burst my throat apart.

HELEN: Make any effort to look devotional at least.

MARY: I'm going to say my piece.

ROSE: Do not risk it for sake of a moment's irritation.

MARY: I don't need lessons in moralising from you, Rose Clarke, I'll do as I please. Verily, I say unto you that man not only wants power over woman but over life. His attraction for lust, power and violence is fatally entwined.

HELEN: Hush, I can hear his footfalls.

MARY: You must be a bat then. Rain has not stopped since harvest. He'll be paddling on mud.

HELEN (*sings boldly*): The Lord's my shepherd I'll not want. He maketh me to lie down in pastures green, he leadeth me the quiet waters.

She stops abruptly as the door opens revealing JANE, *a woman disguised as a soldier.*

MARY (*continuing where* HELEN *leaves off*): Wherein to drown.

ROSE (*surprised to see a soldier*): Oh, and who might you be?

JANE: And who might you be expecting?

MARY: Not you.

HELEN: This is a devotional meeting, sir. For women alone.

JANE: Ha. You'll be thanking Lord Jesus for that then.

ROSE: We have no account to make to you.

JANE *remains where she is and* ROSE *continues to study her during the following dialogue.*

HELEN (*quickly, wanting to pacify*): We are but bald women, sir, asking for God to look down on us in his mercy.

JANE (*heartily*): You look neither useless nor hairless to me.

HELEN: As ye must know, sir, t'is a quirk of our speech that the word for barren and useless be but the same.

ROSE (*sharply*): What business have you here?

JANE: I am a soldier.

MARY (*sarcastically*): Even that much the weaker sex are able to guess at.

HELEN (*kindly*): What can be your enquiry? This is Master Grimbold country . . .

JANE: I have some information which I am in two minds as to if I should impart it to you.

HELEN: Please leave us be.

JANE: Is a question of my sincerity then? Cam now you can trust me.

MARY: Aye, 'tis those assurances have led us to the gallows.

Silence.

ROSE: I am mad for I will say it. Is my guess you be either a vision or a woman.

JANE: Curses! 'Tis the first time I have been tumbled. Now, you have spoilt my revelations.

MARY (*in disbelief*): A woman?

JANE: In truth. Doing a man's job for a man's wage.

HELEN: A woman?

JANE: Aye.

Pause.

ROSE (*coldly*): And what of this information or was it merely a revelation regarding your wardrobe?

JANE: Hovel some distance from here with a tree hanging over, containing an old woman with a fierce mouth.

ROSE: Grace? Would be Grace. (*Concerned.*) What of her?

JANE: Seems she had a visitor cam to frighten her. Mind, she had banished him well afore I got close.

ROSE: And she?

JANE: She was well enough to spit in my direction leading me to conclude she wasn't too weakened by it.

ROSE (*shakes her head*): Can't be Grace. She'd not spit at a brave woman.

JANE: With other things to think on. She took me on face of my apparel.

MARY (*sadly*): Oh for shame of it. I was bad mouthing to her.

JANE: Aye. I'm bound that be but half the tale.

HELEN: To my relief she's cam to no harm. For I must take leave now.

MARY: Where does your husband think you are?

HELEN (*didn't want* MARY *to mention her husband in front of* JANE. *She says casually*): He'd not notice, he's keeping an all-night vigil against the divel. But of my own accord I must take leave. (*To* JANE:) But my hope is that our paths will cross again, Mistress err . . .

JANE: Jane.

HELEN: I'm Helen.

ROSE: Rose.

MARY: Mary.

HELEN: I'll bid you goodnight. (*She goes.*)

JANE: Goodnight.

MARY: All night vigil against the divil. Ha! He'll not be so engrossed that her presence won't be missed when his belly rumbles.

JANE (*checking she has their names right*): Rose. Mary. Do sound like a herb.

ROSE: T'is Grace you should ask about that. Cam on.

They go.

Scene Three

GRACE's *home.*

It is not a hovel, although it is sparse and has a hole in the roof. A pet frog is kept in a box in a corner of the room. GRACE *is plucking a dead chicken. There are numerous jars and bottles containing every sort of herb around.*

GRACE (*mumbles angrily*): You wreck our lives leaving us no recourse but to curse, for which we are condemned. We go to the scaffold cursing for the crime of cursing and would take only a chicken with life wrung from it to be silent from cursing at the injustice of it all.

Enter JANE, MARY *and* ROSE.

ROSE: Is us Grace.

GRACE (*lunging at* JANE *with the chicken carcass*): Do this look like a place stuffed with Royals. Be off with you.

ROSE (*standing between* JANE *and* GRACE): Don't take on, Grace — this, afore your eyes, be a woman. (*Slight pause but* GRACE *doesn't react.*) By name of Jane.

GRACE: What's she doing prynked out like a prick-eared cull?

MARY: For the war — is it not the most wondrous sight?

ROSE (*proudly*): A female soldier, wager you'd not thought you'd live to see the day.

GRACE: Par — you young women. There's no hope.

ROSE (*teasingly*): What relief to find your spirit unruffled by your visitation.

GRACE: I have righted mess he made. Though, warrant, this neutered cock has seen its day. 'Tis only small misfortune and we can make good by it. Pass that pot, Mary.

MARY (*in doing so she sees the frog*): Oh, no Grace, you don't still keep that frog.

GRACE: Good enough for most folks around here. Good enough for me.

JANE: In London they only keep cats and dogs.

GRACE: Cats and dogs cost dear to feed. Many's the time children go without while animals grow fat and full.

MARY: Asides, where would they get frogs from in London?

JANE: They have a fine river you know.

ROSE (*firmly*): We ent assembled here to bend our ears over who's got a frog or not.

JANE: I hear tell in France they eat frogs.

GRACE: Ha. Then I wish he would have took it into his skull to do away with the frog then. T'would have been a fair treat to see him climbing and jumping round the walls trying to grab and strangle it.

ROSE: Frogs! Frogs! Frogs! Is not frogs we're concerned for.

GRACE: Would have broke my heart to loose old croker.

ROSE (*impatiently*): What was *his* purpose?

GRACE (*quietly*): He has got his courage up. Seems I am not so far off next choice to swim. (*Silence.*) Well, is not so remarkable, merely the same road as several of my years have trod before me.

MARY: Hasn't he made enough money from these parts?

ROSE (*gently*): So how cam he left you?

GRACE: Not bargained for the dish of tongues I served him. Made off in a rush of great frustration.

JANE: Wager he'll be back.

MARY (*flatly*): What a comfort you turned out to be.

ROSE: She be right well enough though.

MARY (*panicking*): So what are we to do?

JANE (*brashly, one hand on her sword*): I'll stand behind the door and slice his brain-pan off his shoulders.

ROSE (*with admiration*): Did I not tell you she was a good woman. Is she not a good woman Grace?

GRACE: Rose!

MARY: Such as stars hang in the sky then so should we.

GRACE: And another pricker wilt up in the place of his martyred master.

ROSE: Aye. He'll not be 'man enough' to return hisself so soon. Most probably pay a man tricked out like the divel.

JANE (*cheerfully*): My cuttle don't care which prick's head it cuts off.

GRACE: Their tools, mistress, are best kept from them. Tis not our way.

ROSE: And what pray is our way? (*Sarcastically:*) Cast a spell?

GRACE: Rose, how many times will you need telling not to lark in such a sour humour.

ROSE: So how are we to prepare ourselves for when the divel cams knocking.

GRACE: This business of carnal copulation with Satan is all new.

MARY (*shakes her head*): The curse of printing. Ideas spread faster than the plague.

GRACE: Printing is not the curse but them who decide what's on the lines.

JANE: I have heard tell of a pamphlet which shows more truth of the writers' blighted minds than of women's nature.

MARY: And what do you know of their working pattern?

JANE: A man pricked out as the divel cam to alone old woman and does say, 'I am the divel and I am cam to sleep with thee'. Aye, it sound like a noddy idea but 'tis enough to frighten many out of their wits. And if but a fly cam within arm's length will be proof enough of imps, but is when he stabs her flesh over and over with a blunt nail to find marks of the divel, do most give in.

GRACE: Aye, the pricker's not so called for nothing.

ROSE: Is little use us sat recounting our plight, we must prepare for his entrance. (ROSE *opens the door a little to keep watch.*)

MARY: Save your breath to tell us how.

GRACE: Laughing.

ROSE: Laughing?

GRACE: Aye. 'Tis my new plan. To laugh.

MARY (*flatly*): I don't feel like laughing.

GRACE: Takes courage beyond man to carry out duties amidst raucous ridicule.

JANE: Take a courageous man carry out his duties with a rum cuttle ran through him. (*She puts her hand to her sword.*)

GRACE: That war's done you no good, girl. Now, this is the plan. You three climb up the tree outside and observe scene through unmended hole in the roof.

MARY: Oh Grace, Thatcher still not cam.

GRACE: Thatcher don't care 'bout poor folk on parish welfare.

ROSE: For mercy's sake, I can hear horse hoofs.

GRACE: Signal be, if he so much as poke his finger in my direction — laugh.

ROSE: Right. (*She bundles* MARY *and* JANE *out of the door.*)

MARY: But . . . grace. (ROSE *pushes her.*) But Rose.

ROSE: Get up that tree. (*They all climb into the tree.*)

MARY: But Rose. Point is, we have nothing to laugh at.

ROSE (*whispers*): Shush. (*She points off.*) There he is.

JANE (*whispers*): Worry not on that matter. I know something their adled brains think we do that will make you giggle till your bladders give way.

ROSE: What?

JANE: 'Tis not so funny in second telling. So wait for signal but be warned not to heed your aching sides but cling firmly to these branches.

Disguised as the devil, the Pricker's Apprentice has tethered his horse and walks the rest of the distance. Although this is his first mission, he has been well primed and is confident that his mere presence will scare GRACE *half to death. Consequently he is unnerved by her response.*

APPRENTICE (*enters, announcing grandly*): I am the divel and I am cam to sleep with thee.

GRACE: If the divel has desires for the flesh he must be made of blood and bone.

APPRENTICE (*not the reaction he'd expected; still he must try harder*): I see you have several familiars.

GRACE (*pulling the chicken out of the pot*): You be telling me you be the divel and yer never spied a capon before. Now there's a thing.

APPRRENTICE (*confused now, so more aggressively*): I am cam for a place in your soul.

GRACE: Stop making a cod's head of yourself, man. Behave and take thyself off.

APPRENTICE (*taking a step nearer*): Don't prank with me, I am the divel.

GRACE: So maybe you think you are. Delusions of this nature, especially of men believing themselves to be a character from the Bible are not uncommon. Would it be a relief to talk about this affliction?

APPRENTICE (*is now hard pressed for things the devil might say*): You are in my pay.

GRACE: Well, truth to say, I've received none of it to date. I am a healing woman, a good one but a poor one.

APPRENTICE: Oh shut thy twittering. (*He advances another step closer.*)

GRACE: And *pray* — oh, I see that word don't shock you none. What have I done that you should pester me so?

APPRENTICE: You are evil.

GRACE: The divel is calling a mere mortal evil?

APPRENTICE: I'll teach you to mock my powers.

He tries to grab her but she nimbly avoids him.

JANE (*to* MARY *and* ROSE): They are of firm belief that women collect male organs and keep them in birds' nests where they move about by themselves and eat corn and oats.

The three of them screech with laughter.

APPRENTICE: What is this divlery? (*He hesitates. The laughter continues.*)

GRACE: Run along with you, mister, and tell who ever's paying you there's no business for him here.

The Pricker's Apprentice turns tail and swiftly exits. When he is out of sight, MARY, ROSE *and* JANE *descend from the tree and return to* GRACE *who is tending to the stew.*

ROSE: A wondrous plan, Grace.

MARY: Aye, my face is wet from laughing.

GRACE: You have some peculiar ideas, young Jane but I'll like you yet, and you took a risk revealing yourself to the meeting.

JANE: I have a text, Grace. 'Where two or three women are gathered together t'is a risk worth taking.'

ROSE: Tell us of the war.

JANE: The war? The war, Rose, is a fuckin' bore. Tonight I'm more interested in the conflict around your necks and the purpose of your meeting.

ROSE: The idea belongs to Grace.

MARY: We're trying to put some words together so we can perform them.

JANE: I've not heard of women doing that.

ROSE: We'd not heard of women passing as men till today.

JANE: And when?

MARY: At next lying-in.

JANE: For what purpose?

GRACE: Is the only time women are allowed to be together.

ROSE: So we can feel less afraid of these evil times against our sex.

JANE: How can it be women of our time are stronger than ever before and yet persecuted worse at same time?

GRACE: When those who are accumbred kick back, the oppressor kicks harder.

JANE: But they pick on frail, defenceless old women. Oh begging your pardon, Grace, but usually by their very age they can offer least resistance.

GRACE: First there is your reason, is easy. Second, some have power, such as they see it in health and advice over women's bodies, particularly in child-bearing. And they want power over that.

MARY: Only there's not enough of a complex nature about their own bodies to keep their minds occupied.

JANE: But the doctors are not the prickers.

GRACE: New inventions and persecution step together, in time.

ROSE: At least they're not hypocrites and do call themselves doctors.

JANE (*confused*): I know not what the word means.

ROSE: To cut up. To doctor — to tamper with in an unnatural way.

JANE: So then — put a stop to me if you've heard it — This doctor goes to a cunning woman with a frog on his head and the cunning woman asks, 'How long have you had that?' and the frog says, 'Long since it started as an abcess on my arse'.

They all laugh including JANE.

GRACE: I see, if nothing else, you have some store of jokes in your head, mistress.

JANE: Aye, well, I know this much. T'will be a long time afore the likes of us have money for a doctor to lay his hand on doorpost never mind else.

MARY: And who do you think they'll practise on?

JANE: I'm not so easily convinced, I've heard tell . . .

GRACE: You seem to have heard tell a lot for a woman of your years.

JANE: The war, Grace, it gets you around. Is best education a girl can have.

GRACE: Par – Glory and killing would seem to my mind to lead to dead end.

JANE: In France.

ROSE: France? How d'you know about France?

JANE: Loyalist always going there.

GRACE (*slightly mocking*): Oh aye and they confide in you?

JANE: I am nobody's halfwit. I have change of clothes and curls under this headpiece. I choose safest disguise depending on company I keep.

GRACE: Probably you're keeping war going single-handed.

ROSE (*prompting* JANE): So in France . . .

JANE: In their history they did burn four hundred women in town square in one hour all over country and many low countries besides. Whole villages left with one woman. Just one alive. Was not the doctors' doing, was the church.

Silence.

GRACE: Certainly sad to say t'was better when we was all Catholics. At least Virgin Mary was sacred. There's not a good word to be said for Eve. Though where men reason they cam from if not Eve, I don't know.

ROSE: They name the name, if it don't fit they name it again.

GRACE: It won't stop. Not here nor now. Will not stop till they can give birth and then have choice to do away with us altogether.

JANE (*laughs*): Oh aye Grace. And when will that be? Before or after they walk on the moon?

GRACE, MARY, ROSE, JANE *sing*:
And a Man Named Armstrong Walked Upon the Moon

So you think that's an ironic joke?
At NASA's celestial poke.
They thrust up a man into space,
  But you won't even think
  That they're on the brink
Of finishing off half our race.

For women have the bodies that breed
And the men just provide her the seed
So love guides the stars in our eyes,
  With feet on the earth,
  Men can't control birth,
And a man on the moon is all lies.

For men have ejaculated onto the moon
By rocket, and phallic intent
Has given new meaning to that old
  famous rune
That for men's domination the great
  moon was meant.

There's a warning here, sisters, let's
  take heed of this,
That man on the moon came to earth:
And fucking and love may start with a
  kiss
And you may control your kids' birth
But not for long now, they're taking
  our place.
Fashioning Star Wars in labs. Winning
  the race
To eradicate us and give birth by men
Fashioning new wombs inside of them.
So don't laugh at the technological joke
Of scientists' long-reaching poke
They're doing the same thing now
  with their reproductive technology
And Neil Armstrong gives the Man in
  the Moon no apology.

Scene Four
Outside.
  The same night. Behind an inn. A
WOMAN, *hands tied behind her back,*
feet bound, is slumped in a cart. Her
daughter, URSULA, *watches from a*
distance. When she perceives no one

else is around she runs to her MOTHER, *lightly jumps onto the cart and starts to untie her hands.* URSULA *was born deaf. She makes no sound when she communicates but uses sign language and mouths the words simultaneously.*

MOTHER: Oh child, go. Go back lest they find you here.

URSULA, *having untied her* MOTHER'*s hands, proceeds to loosen the ropes around her feet.*

(*Knocking* URSULA'*s hands away*:) No, no, it's of no use. (*She holds out her hands, which are numb.*) My hands are all but dead. Where rope has bitten into them.

URSULA *starts to rub her* MOTHER'*s hands until she can flex her fingers, then she goes to untie her feet. Taking* URSULA'*s hands away, her* MOTHER *speaks softly, signing at the same time:*

Is no good. Go now and save yourself.

URSULA (*signs*): Cam, cam back with me.

MOTHER (*continuing to sign as she speaks*): I cannot. My leg is broken. Is too painful.

URSULA *brings out a leather bottle from her skirts. Her* MOTHER *angrily snatches it away from her and throws it to the ground.*

What did I counsel you? You know nothing of herbs or healing. Remember nothing.

URSULA *holds her* MOTHER'*s head in her shoulder.*

(*To herself:*) Better to let the water take me and give them proof of my innocence. They cannot then cam looking for you. Born deaf to them is sign of divel's work.

She gently lifts URSULA'*s head, so that she can sign and says:*

Go to the big house and I will pray the lady take pity on you and give you work. Quickly afore my gaoler return from his ale-drinking.

URSULA *lingers.*

Please go now.

She kisses URSULA *and then gently pushes her away.* URSULA *looks at her* MOTHER, *turns, jumps down from the cart and runs.*

(*To herself:*) Please God keep her safe. Spare her.

Scene Five

The pond.

GRACE, ROSE, HELEN *and* MARY *stand on the edge of a large crowd. All that can be seen is the cross-bar of the gallows with the top of the rope hanging from it. At the moment the box is kicked away they turn and face outwards, eyes down, unable to look at each other, isolated by a sense of powerlessness and grief.* GRACE, HELEN *and* MARY *go off in different directions. The only sound is that of the rope straining against the wood.* ROSE *is alone. She sits as far away from the scene as possible and picks up two stones, idly knocking them together. Enter a fellow worker, a* MAN.

MAN: That be a fine way to spend an afternoon off now, Rose. Cam. Let's make the best of the sunshine and take us a stroll together. (*Silence.*) Maybe I'm not earning up to your expectation and it be the farmer hisself you're hoping for, eh?

ROSE, *fists flying, goes for him.*

He steps out of the way, laughing.

Oh, I'll have to be telling the pricker I've found one that can fly without a broomstick. Heh, heh.

He wanders off still chuckling. She throws the stones ineffectually after him and then sits down again. URSULA *enters, unseen by* ROSE, *stands some distance away, trying to summon the courage to approach* ROSE.

ROSE (*becoming aware that she is being watched, turns*): Who are you? (URSULA *doesn't move.*) Don't worry, I won't fly at you. What do you want with me? (*Pause.*) Well, if you don't speak up how am I to know? ROSE *turns back and resumes staring ahead.* URSULA *takes a couple of steps towards* ROSE *but sees* JANE *approaching and takes fright and goes off.* JANE *sits next to* ROSE.

JANE (*gloomily*): Seems we didn't give his apprentice fright enough. (*Then:*) What are you doing sat there, Rose?

ROSE (*flatly*): Waiting for the stars to cam out.

JANE: Won't right yourself by sulking. Is not *your* tongue that has been stopped in your throat today.

ROSE: Easy words for you. Who was it spoke out last time? Grace.

JANE: Aye. (*Pause.*) I'd like to see her again afore I go.

ROSE: Go? When?

JANE: With the sun. And hoping it will prompt me to rise afore I'm missed.

ROSE: But I will see you again.

JANE: That be another thing I am hoping for.

ROSE: Can I get word to you?

JANE: Via another soldier perhaps. Though messages are apt to be long forgotten afore they arrive to those receiving them.

ROSE: I will write to you.

JANE (*incredulously*): You can write?

ROSE: Aye, and read.

JANE: You can read and write?

ROSE: Aye. Can you not hear under that helmet?

JANE: But how?

ROSE: Oft I go over to Grace and we stay awake all night. Her teaching me. Mind, is hard to set to work the next day without falling asleep over my pail.

JANE: Grace can read and write too?

ROSE: Course. I didn't learn from air. When her father saw he wasn't to have no sons, he taught her instead. She knows all manner of things that she taught herself besides.

JANE: Like what?

ROSE: Names and properties of herbs and plants and different ways to help heal the body.

JANE: So tell me about them.

ROSE: All that be of more interest to Grace than me. But I know the names of the stars.

JANE: So what are thay?

ROSE: I can't show you now, can I? (*Pointing to the sky.*)

JANE (*carefully casual*): Maybe if we couldst meet at night you'd tell me.

ROSE: About best one is named Ursa Major.

JANE: Never heard of it.

ROSE: It means the Great Bear.

JANE: You ever seen a real bear?

ROSE: I cannot say I have.

JANE: I have, some miles back, chained up in an inn garden.

ROSE: A bear?

JANE: Aye.

ROSE: A proper bear? A live bear?

JANE: Aye. (*Teasingly:*) Maybe you'd like to borrow my helmet to aid your hearing.

ROSE (*jumping to her feet*): Meet me here as sun goes down. I've got a new plan. (*She starts to go.*)

JANE (*disappointed*): You mean we're not going to look at stars together after all.

Scene Six

Outside.

Night. ROSE *and* JANE *lead or rather are lead down the street towards the*

PRICKER's *house by a dancing* BEAR.

ROSE: My hope is that Grace is late. I didn't find courage enough to tell her about this.

JANE: She'll be pleased with us right enough. Surely.

ROSE: We don't even know if our friend Ursa is male or female.

JANE: Well, I ent getting down on my hands and knees in the dark to have a look. Should it make a difference?

ROSE: It might to Grace. She don't hold with violence for our sex.

JANE: What do she hold with for bears?

ROSE: I don't rightly know.

JANE (*unconcerned*): We're sure to find out by and by.

ROSE (*worried*): I don't doubt.

JANE: Look, I don't hold with violence myself (ROSE *looks at her in disbelief*:) against our sex and that is for why Ursa must try and kill him and nature take its course and the blame. Now quit worrying Rose. Look at it − not stopped dancing all the way − most probably be too wore out to piss.

ROSE: S'pose then it don't kill him?

JANE: At very least it will give him shock enough to soil his breeches.

ROSE: My hope is, t'is not accustomed to being shut behind door and t'will run amok.

JANE (*pointing*): That is pricker's residence, is it not?

ROSE: S'pose . . .

JANE: Now ent time for s'posing, now's the time for doing.

JANE *opens the door, puts her shoulder against the* BEAR's *back and shoves it inside.* ROSE *and* JANE *then crouch beneath the window. The* BEAR *lumbers towards the* PRICKER *and sits on the end of the bed. The* PRICKER *remains asleep. After a*

moment ROSE *puts her head on the window sill.*

JANE (*whispers*): What is it? Has the shock laid him out dead?

ROSE: I'm surprised the shock ain't laid the bear out dead. It just slumped on the bed. Not even awoke the pricker.

JANE *gets up and shuts the door with an almighty slam, then runs back and crouches under the window.*

PRICKER (*wakes, startled*): What the? Who's there? Who is it?

ROSE (*deep booming voice*): I am the biggest imp of all and I am cam to be familiar to you.

The PRICKER *jumps out of bed, screaming.* JANE *pulls* ROSE *down.*

PRICKER: Leave me be. Leave me be. (*He tears around the room in a mad panic, screaming, the* BEAR *loping after him.*)

JANE (*puts her head up, to* ROSE): Oh no, the lumping great noddy has put its arm round him. (*In a deep voice*:) The divel has sent me for you are his most trusted worker.

JANE *ducks down.* ROSE *puts her head up. The screams reach an unbearable pitch as the* BEAR *tries to dance with the* PRICKER.

ROSE: Oh no. It's trying to dance with him.

JANE *sinks down as the* PRICKER *frees himself from the* BEAR's *grasp, jumps through the window and runs, without looking behind, until he is out of sight.*

JANE (*gleefully*): Well, that's that.

ROSE (*giggles*): Leastways he won't be queueing up to stay in that room again in a hurry.

JANE: And we don't have to worry about sex of the bear for it did only dance and I'm sure even Grace holds with dancing.

ROSE: I have no mind about that now.

Fact I wish it had done away with him.

Enter GRACE.

GRACE: Look at you pair of leverets, giving yourself hemorodes under the pricker's nose.

ROSE: Grace. Oh, Grace, you just missed picture of a lifetime.

GRACE: Get yourselves off that wet grass afore you grow any protrusions that he'll use as evidence of imp suckling. Is that I cannot bear.

JANE: Now, I'm glad you brung bears into the conversation.

ROSE: Pricker has fled.

GRACE (*confused*): Bears? Pricker fled?

JANE (*halfway through the window*): Cam, look for yourself. (JANE *and* ROSE *help* GRACE *through the window.*) Well, has made good use of bed. Is asleep.

ROSE: Best day's work it's ever done, in moons I'll warrant. More the shame that it never gobbled him up.

GRACE *laughs.*

JANE: We thought you'd be vexed at plan, not laughing.

GRACE: Brown bears are vegetarians.

ROSE: Are what?

GRACE: Only eat greens. Turn nose up at flesh.

JANE (*defensively*): Well, it danced with him.

GRACE: It would have been trained by players to do that.

JANE: Well, it don't look like it's about to take a bow. It won't budge. And I'm loathe to prod it in case it turns on us.

ROSE (*pointing*): And it can't sleep there a night or we're done for.

GRACE: Let's find some edible foliage suitable to its diet in pricker's garden. And we'll lure it out.

JANE: Leave me to rummage through this pit. There may be papers of interest to you, Grace.

ROSE *and* GRACE *leave the room.* JANE *makes a search of the room and finds a sum of money hidden under some papers. She hesitates. Looks up, but* ROSE *and* GRACE *aren't watching so she puts the money inside her jerkin.* ROSE *and* GRACE *come back inside the room armed with lettuce leaves.*

ROSE: You find anything?

JANE (*holds up some papers*): These, but I can't choose which to take, on account of I can't read.

GRACE: Let me see.

ROSE: Take them, Grace. We dare not wait here longer.

GRACE *takes the papers and waves the leaves under the* BEAR's *nose. It wakes up and nibbles at them.*

JANE: See, all it wanted was a nap.

GRACE *entices the* BEAR *out of the room.*

ROSE: Must be feeling sorry for itself that it's dancing partner was so unsuitable.

When they are all outside.

GRACE: Would be best course to return this noble creature while its owners still slumber.

JANE: I am headed in that same direction and will be thankful in morning to have curtailed my travelling distance.

ROSE: But . . .

JANE: And none of your protests for it would be foolhardy man who attacked a soldier with a bear for a guard.

ROSE: Will we see you again?

JANE: When is next meeting?

GRACE: Not till full moon.

JANE: So t'is true covens meet by full moon.

ROSE: How else can you see foot in front of ditch?

JANE: If I'm still drawing breath and sword I'll hope to attend.

Exit JANE *pursued by a sleepy* BEAR.

GRACE: That is either a very hammer-headed woman or a very brave one.

ROSE: T'is a bit of both to my reckoning but that don't alter my opinion of her one jot.

GRACE (*laughs*): Aye.

GRACE *and* ROSE *continue on their way in silence.*

GRACE (*cheerfully*): You've not got a lot to say for one just performed historic service to womankind.

ROSE (*flatly*): I am pleased enough.

Silence.

GRACE (*sits down on a tree stump*): Cam on girl, spit it up.

ROSE (*sitting down next to* GRACE): Surely there are more problems facing us than brown bears left in the world.

GRACE (*smiles*): When did you learn to place such melancholy humour in your turn of phrase? Surely we can afford to smile at our triumphs?

ROSE: I want you to make a potion for me.

GRACE (*concerned*): Oh Rose, I knew not. Who did get away with that?

ROSE: Nay, not that. Though is connected but not in a straight-line way.

GRACE: What is? The hour is late and I have no eye to see into your brain.

ROSE: Is difficult.

GRACE: Aye.

ROSE: I do not want to grow into a woman.

GRACE *laughs.*

(*Angrily:*) Is not something to ache your jaw over. (*Then calmly:*) I am not womanly enough for farmer's liking but soon as I becam ripe enough for all to see he'll pluck me too. I eat so little, Grace, I would rather wilt than grow.

GRACE: That course can only do you harm. Short of poisoning yourself there is no way halt you becoming a woman.

ROSE: Sometime he cam so close I feel his breath on back of my neck and have to cast up behind a tree.

GRACE: That be customary put off. The farmer is the problem not your body.

ROSE: Easy words. For I hate him. I hate the work. And I hate my body also.

GRACE: You been on earth long enough to know choices are few. Least milking cows keep you free from pox.

ROSE: Milking farmer won't keep me free of other pox.

Silence.

GRACE: I am old woman now. I can't live forever.

ROSE: Don't say that Grace. As if I am not maudlin enough.

GRACE: Is a truth you'd best prepare for. I'd be honoured to teach you about the herbs and matters for body's well-being such as I know.

ROSE (*bursts out*): Oh no Grace! I don't want to know none of that. I am best not knowing. I have plenty more preference for making a play than a child. Be the worst thing that could happen to me and I would rather be on parish or in stocks than tend women in labour — yeuk, how could you suggest such a thing?

GRACE: These things seem not vital when you're young and have rude health.

ROSE: That has nothing to do with it. I tell you, Grace. I hate mere thought of touching bodies never mind else. Don't ever speak of it again to me.

GRACE (*sadly*): Rose.

ROSE: I won't blight this day with any more talk of it. Cam now, let's make off to Ann and Mary.

GRACE: Have we not put ourselves in enough danger this night?

ROSE: We have a lucky star to protect us.

GRACE: Oh aye?

ROSE: Make cheerful, for these dumps have left me. If I can make a plan to rid us of pricker, can only be a matter of time afore I do away with farmer.

They go.

Enter DOCTOR.

DOCTOR (*sings*):

God and the Technodoc

What is life but for creating
    Other life to carry on,
Churches and religion taught us
    We are made to marry one
Who like God can create babies
    Embryos of human form,
Where is life and science going
    Who decides the foetal norm?

Medicine is a new religion
    Opium to the childless pair
Who can judge when what's on offer
    Gives to them an equal share
Of the right to bring forth babies
    Perfect creatures shaped by man,
What will happen to the others
    Miscarried in the master plan.

Eradicate all forms of illness,
    Handicap and brain disease?
No one will be born disabled
    The technodoc is out to please.
Join the doctors and the medics,
    Scientists of the human life
Babies are essential for them
    To sustain the perfect wife.

Science has at its disposal
    Power to reproduce the race.
All the kindly interventions
    Are the subtle saving face
Of the other side of medicine.
    Interference is the plan.

Making life by experimentation
    Women's bodies controlled by man.

The DOCTOR *goes.*

Scene Seven

The servants' attic in LADY H*'s house.*
    MARY *and* ANN *are sewing, mending a variety of garments from an assortment scattered around them.*

MARY (*stopping to rub her eyes*): Is no good, Ann, I will have to sleep else when morning comes my eyes will resemble two pissholes in the snow.

ANN: Sshush, don't make so much noise.

MARY: I am sewing as quietly as I can. (*She grins.*)

ANN: You'll be grinning when Lady Wipe-my-arse catches you awake at this hour.

MARY: She has never caught me awake or in any other position at this hour. (*Then:*) Aye. This day hast been bitter enough. Let's shut our eyes on it.

ANN: If we was to keep vigil for every woman killed we'd not get sleep for many years hence.

MARY: Aye. (*She yawns.*)

ANN: Our time will come for their accusations and you cannot shut your eyes on that.

MARY: I have said I will mind child whilst you can go to the meetings.

ANN: All you do there is argue over who does it right way or wrong way — I'd rather keep my precious free time to myself.

MARY: Is not all like that. Asides is important to sort out differences.

ANN: Seem a mighty luxury to my mind. Risking everything to meet, causing you to be half-asleep at your work. We are not granted privilege of living quarters big enough to stand up in, never mind liberty to run around the village half the night. If you are caught will only confirm their suspicions that you are up to no good.

MARY: We cannot do nothing.

ANN: On that we are agreed, so we must leave.

MARY: Would be treacherous, we have no money.

ANN: As if I know not that. For if we did we'd not be sat here tickling each other's ears about it. I know it be a gamble we must take.

MARY: Gamble? Sheer peril. And what of the child?

ANN: You let me worry over the child. I am her mother.

MARY: Don't start that up.

ANN: You are the one most free to go and yet is you who are most scared. Can you not understand our safety here hangs by a thread.

MARY: We'd not find a position like we have here.

ANN: So it's not Grace nor Rose nor the rest keeping you here but the high time you have in your master's house.

MARY: With a footman and stable boy who are partial to each other and they are happy to keep up pretence of a bogus alliance with us to keep themselves from prying eyes. We would not find another position so favourable.

ANN: Bachelors aren't hung for their sex.

MARY: Ones of their leanings are neither embraced by their fellows. Cook says she heard talk of a cunning woman who arranges sham marriages between folks like us. So we can carry on our lives as we wish without tongues wagging.

ANN: What might you be suggesting now? That we all bed down together?

MARY: Merely that, is safer here than you s'pose.

ANN: I have no faith that when the rope grips our throats we shall hear but even a squeak of rebuke from either footman or stable boy.

A knock at the door makes them start. They both stand. MARY *picks up a piece of wood.*

(*Behind the door*): Who is it?

ROSE: Rose and Grace.

ANN (*opening the door, ushering them into the room*): What trouble has brought you here at this hour?

GRACE: No trouble. Set your mind at rest.

ROSE (*shouts*): We have rid . . .

MARY: Quietly now for we cannot afford whole household to know our affairs.

ROSE (*grandly*): We have rid this place this very night of the pricker.

ANN: How? (*Delighted.*) Rose, how?

ROSE. We frighted him with a bear. (*Pause for effect.*) A dancing bear.

MARY: I can guess whose cunning was behind that.

GRACE: Oh no. All young Rose's doing.

ROSE: And Jane.

MARY: Aye, from the moment I set eyes on her I knew she had spirit.

ANN (*smiles at* MARY): Jane? And who might she be?

MARY: That young mistress dressed as a soldier.

ROSE (*to* MARY): Aye and the moment you laid eyes on her you thought she was a man.

ANN: So, is he dead?

ROSE: No.

GRACE (*sharply*): Rose!

ROSE (*she looks at* GRACE): Aye and perhaps that is best. But is my guess he will not show his face round here lest the vision of his massive grizzly imp haunt him.

GRACE: Will mean a new start.

MARY: Do you hear that, Ann?

ANN: Aye. (*With delight.*) We are free. We are free.

Enter LADY AITCH (LADY H). *She barges into the centre of the room and so has her back towards* ROSE. *They are all rather shocked and a bit frightened by her presence.*

LADY H: There is more of you than I remembered.

MARY: If it please, my lady, these are two women from the village who are err . . . cam to err . . .

ROSE (*quickly*): Give the child lucky charm for its christening.

LADY H: Strange rituals.

GRACE: No, Lady H, t'was a present. Not a charm. Rose, we do not want Lady H to believe we are ignorant, superstitious people.

ROSE (*mutters*): What we want don't come into it.

ROSE *and* GRACE *make to leave.*

LADY H: No, please, don't leave. I have had some sorry news. Seems my husband's guts got spilled in battle.

ROSE (*from behind* LADY H's *back holds up two fingers and mouths*): Two down.

MARY: We are sad for your distress, my lady.

LADY H: He was away much anyway but there are certain responsibilities I cannot take unaided.

ANN: That is sorry news, my lady.

LADY H: Rumour hath reached my ears that meetings happen in the village for women without menfolk and, further, you attend them.

ANN: Only at night, my lady and we do not sleep in your work.

LADY H: That I am not disputing, though God knows I should be. I am enquiring as to when, so that I might join you.

ROSE: You would not care for them, lady, we are a very rough crowd.

MARY: Begging your pardon, but I don't see how they could help you, with all respect.

LADY H: But I am given to understand that each gains solace for your life's lost happiness and further find husbands for one another and other lonely widows.

ANN: You would not like it.

LADY H: How am I to judge until. . . .

GRACE: We know of no men suiting to your station and your ladyship would not care to be married off to any old cobbler would she?

LADY H: Certainly not.

Pause.

Alas, I am so confused, and in your debt for righting me. I have quite forgot my status. I'll bid you all goodnight.

(*She turns. Then as an afterthought*:) Oh Ann, cam and see me first thing in the morning. I will need you to wetnurse the youngest heir. I am much too hard pressed for time myself.

She goes.

ANN (*ironically*): Now, where were we? Oh, yes, as we were saying. We are free.

Scene Eight

The meeting room.
GRACE, ROSE, HELEN *and* MARY.

ROSE (*to* HELEN): Least you can do is open your mouth and give us a half-good word of praise.

HELEN: You shad never have done such a thing, Rose. He'll only be more vengeful than afore.

ROSE: You have faith he'd have stopped afore we was all rotted at bottom of the pond?

HELEN: You've placed the rest of our lives in jeopardy.

ROSE: They was in jeopardy anyway.

GRACE: Leave her be, Helen. The pricker has not been seen since. Was a very brave thing Rose done.

ROSE: And Jane.

MARY (*teasing* ROSE): Oh aye and Jane.

HELEN: Fine for Jane, being as she's not from here. No nail or noose will reach her — a mere lark to her mind.

ROSE (*losing her temper*): Don't you go putting her under. You a fine one to say such things yourself. No one cam looking for you, being married as you are. I am cam to accept that I would never get a pat on the head or back from you but you never open your mouth except to drench other's suggestions.

MARY: I agree on that.

GRACE: Let's us get on with the play.

MARY: I'm sick of the bleedin' play. It has taken so long. Will look out of fashion now we have rid ourselves of the evil.

GRACE: We have rid ourselves of all evil, eh?

MARY: Oh, I'm not going to ache my brain reasoning with you, Grace. I'll do my bit so long as Helen promises to keep silent.

GRACE: We have enough wishing that on us in every waking hour to be guarded enough not to ask it of each other.

HELEN (*pathetically*): I cannot help being married. Is difficult to shake off accumbrements of parson.

ROSE: Nobody asked you to marry him.

HELEN: He did.

MARY: You should have said no. You

are not a lady of wealth enough to have it arranged for you.

HELEN: I have always wanted children but it was not to be. Even Grace cannot tell why and it can't be his fault for men of the cloth are not prone to pox.

ROSE: Ha ha.

HELEN (*brightly*): Cam, I am still committed to our endeavours and will hold my tongue still from anything but praise.

GRACE: Right, now, Mary. I hear you have some wonderous new words to add.

MARY (*hesitates but then stands*): 'Verily we enquire!'

Enter JANE.

JANE (*jocular as ever*): Me again, you bundle of old maids, the soldier returned to your arms.

ROSE: You came!

JANE: Flying pitchforks couldn't keep me away. I cannot tarry long.

GRACE: You are in time to see our play.

JANE (*alarmed*): Has the pricker returned then?

ROSE: No. Sent for his belongings and has settled elsewhere.

GRACE: He was but part of our troubles the rest have not vanished.

JANE: Truth to say, that's, in part, reason why I'm stood here. Is about his belongings. I have grown accustomed to poking through purses of dead men and that night when you and Grace was coaxing the bear I found some money in Pricker's house.

She throws it down.

Do not be sore with me for I have righted myself. Is not mine.

GRACE: Nor ours.

JANE: Is now. And I have delayed too long already.

MARY: Surely half the money is yours.

JANE: I want nowt of it. That is my payment to myself for concealing it from such friends. I am away and don't say goodbye for it would not do for a soldier to be seen with misty eyes, for I will see you again soon.

She goes.

GRACE *is about to say something but she has gone. The others sit staring at the money.*

MARY: Really, by rights, it belongs to Rose.

ROSE (*shakes her head*): It is soiled. I did not earn it by torturing women.

HELEN: True place then would be the pondbed.

GRACE: Where it would not even be of benefit to duck's diet. Surely t'is the property of the relatives of the women whose lives paid for it?

MARY: The factor that they had no relatives sped him in his work.

ROSE: Then maybe is ours to share? How much is there, Grace?

GRACE: You can count good as I. See for yourself.

ROSE (*carefully counts it*): Five and twenty shillings.

HELEN: So what does that work out at each?

ROSE: I just managed to count it — do you want miracle from me?

GRACE: Six shillings.

MARY (*whistles*): Six shillings?

GRACE: And threepence, but wait on, aren't we going to use it for something for all of us.

HELEN (*jokingly*): Like what — buy an inn?

GRACE: What do each of you want then?

MARY: Ann would like to go to London and my excuse has all but disappeared with this windfall.

HELEN: That be no place for a child.

MARY: I have told her but it seems women are kicking up great protest there and would be fine thing to be part of. So you, Helen? What would you have?

HELEN: A child.

ROSE (*not nastily*): That might cost you dear but you don't need to part with no money.

HELEN: With money I can afford a doctor from the town.

ROSE: Oh no, tell me my lugs have turned to liars.

HELEN: To me is worth trying.

ROSE: Par. You would willingly give them power over us by offering yourself up for their butchery.

GRACE (*sternly*): Is all right for you Rose. You do not entertain thought of having children but it be a severe mistake to dismiss them what do.

MARY (*gently*): There are plenty of motherless children in the world.

HELEN: But I wish for one of my own. Only what most women take as given. Oh aye, and a great burden to many but t'is something I want for myself. Am I to be denied that?

GRACE (*carefully*): And s'pose there is no cure for you, Helen?

HELEN: Then I will buy a babe.

MARY:
ROSE: } (*outraged*): Buy one!

HELEN: Plenty of women have so many they don't know what to do with them.

MARY: Buy one off Lady H, then. She's always farming them out.

HELEN: Money wouldn't induce her, she don't need it.

GRACE: Aye.

Silence.

MARY: And what then are your dreams, Rose?

ROSE: I will buy some men's clothes and then I'm off to find Jane and fight alongside in the war.

HELEN: But you'll have to charge about with a pike.

ROSE: Is no heavier than a scythe and a lot less wieldy to use.

Pause.

Grace?

GRACE: I am too saddened to reason further.

HELEN: Seems the only thing left is to share it.

ROSE (*goes to pick it up, then*): We've not heard from Grace yet.

MARY: Oh aye. What's it to be for you, Grace?

GRACE: I all but feel out of turn now. For I wanted us to remain together and form a band of travelling players to go from county to country entertaining women . . .

GRACE: Making them laugh, dispelling myths and superstitions and fears so that life and health and well-being were no longer mysteries but understood by one and all.

Silence.

GRACE: Rose?

ROSE: My mind is set but after the war . . .

GRACE: Always taken as given you are living.

ROSE: I want to be equal, Grace. Treated the same.

GRACE: But not in war — in peace. We are becoming stronger, now is not the time to throw it away.

ROSE: I am throwing nothing away 'cept my servitude.

HELEN: We should pledge now to meet two years from hence and find what has becam of our dreams.

Silence.

GRACE: I cannot say goodbye in this room. Let us walk as far as the house together afore we go our separate ways.

MARY (*off*): I can't wait to tell Ann.

HELEN (*off*): I'm not telling Parson.

HELEN *and* MARY *go off.* ROSE *and* GRACE *linger.*

ROSE: You are sorely disappointed in me, Grace?

GRACE: I know well enough once you have idea stuck in your head, take the divil to shift it.

ROSE: I will cam back and when I do I'll have written a play all myself, Grace, for you. I won't forget you.

GRACE *turns away.*

Are you all right?

GRACE: Aye, just tired.

ROSE *takes* GRACE's *arm and they go. Presently* LADY H *enters looking rather the worse for the weather.*

LADY H: Yoo hoo. Cam on now. Show thyselves. I know this is where you meet.

Enter the PRICKER.

PRICKER: I have you now.

LADY H: Ah ha, now are you looking for a woman?

PRICKER: Which woman?

LADY H: Was your intent to pose that as question or accusation?

PRICKER: Oh, begging your pardon. I didn't realise was you, Lady H.

LADY H: Oh, t'is but you, Master er . . . How remiss of me, I cannot recall your name. I thought you'd left this part of the country long since.

PRICKER (*doffs his hat*): Newly

appointed Woman-Finder General and you do well to take my advice, Lady H, and not lurk around this place at night or I might mistake you for a hag.

LADY H: I am apt to overlook your insult as my appearance is somewhat impaired by the elements and I don't suppose with your newly acquired grand title you'll be having much to do with a muddy rut like this village now.

PRICKER: On the contrary. Soon I am to be stationed by here for good. Alas, there is evil in the air.

LADY H: I need no reminding, for why do you think I look like I've been wrestling with a hawthorn bush? As you are so concerned with the air you'd not mind giving me your cape for it's a fair walk back to my house.

She takes the cape before he can protest and goes, leaving him standing alone in the room.

PART TWO

Scene One

Outside.
    Two years later. ROSE, *now a soldier, is on watch duty. She stands alone, occasionally adding a branch or log from the pile of dry wood beside her to the small fire in front of her.* JANE *enters, bounds over to* ROSE *and slaps an arm around her.* ROSE *looks up suprised and pleased and then looks around her nervously.*

JANE: Never worry. They are always slapping arms round each other. Why aren't you down yonder (*Nodding down the hill.*) fighting with the foliage to ferret out the spy.

ROSE: Why aren't you?

JANE: I am to deliver a message and waiting on a fresh horse.

ROSE: Oh.

    Pause.

JANE: To my reckoning this war will soon be finished with.

ROSE: You've been saying that with the same regularity as moon waxing and I know t'is only to keep me cheerful.

JANE: Nay, I do feel it in my bones.

ROSE: We can only pray you don't feel a bullet in your bones as proof of your miscalculation.

JANE: There is much talk of it.

ROSE: And where will they seek their enjoyment and bragging then?

JANE: Is but their bluff and relief on feeling of having cheated death. For if you have lived through the bloodiest battle, the possibility of tripping over a stone and getting a broke neck do seem remote.

ROSE: Par, that explanation be too generous by half.

JANE: So then, and I've been thinking on this, maybe is compensation for their inabilities. Alarmed that they cannot give life they do find glory in death. Surely that serves as explanation enough as to why they oft set themselves dangerous tasks for no other purpose than to prove themselves — t'is envy of birth. There now would not Grace be proud of my reasoning! Maybe could even go in your play.

ROSE: I had a dream of Grace. Seems I was calling out her name — much to all else's amusement.

JANE: If you callest out the name of every woman you know, you'll be gaining a reputation of a real ladies' man.

ROSE: You be almost as bad — you view everything in jest.

JANE: Oh Rosie, you would have me leave with face down to my knees?

ROSE: No, for if you leave I am afraid, and by staying here I am afraid. I do spend all my time in fear.

JANE: Tell me then what is without fear. You can lock your life away behind four walls and still be murdered in your bed.

ROSE: That is of little consolation.

JANE: I do miss you.

ROSE: And supposing we never see each other again?

JANE: Now ain't the time for supposing.

ROSE: Oh and why not?

JANE: Supposing you'd choked to death in your cot, supposing life got crushed out of you by a cow toppling on top of you?

ROSE (*smiles*): The likelihood of that has lost me no sleep.

JANE: Supposing farmer bedded you and you died in childbed? Suppose you'd been swam and hung? Supposed I'd not met you, then we'd not be supposing.

ROSE: Suppose some sword run through your breast.

JANE: Then.

ROSE: Then won't be the time for supposing.

JANE: Where is the bravery of the bear baiter?

ROSE: It got lost in some ditch, or behind some wall. I don't know anymore and if you lay dead or dying I would have no knowledge of that either.

JANE: If I am alive I will find you and if I die I shall remember to do so thinking of you. So you will know and you must do the same for me.

Pause.

Though I don't think you should put that in the play. Would make my character sound damaged in the brain-pan.

ROSE: You silly mome. Is not your character I want to keep alive. Is you. And me.

JANE: I know. Rosie, I know.

JANE *hugs* ROSE. *Enter male* SOLDIER. ROSE *and* JANE's *body language and posture change in front of him. They 'act' and talk like men.*

SOLDIER: I thought you was to keep watch, not cling to each other like a couple of wet nurse-maids.

JANE (*turning to face him*): What business be it of yours?

SOLDIER: Plenty if we are attacked because of your tomfoolery. I am cam through to report, friend, that your horse be ready.

JANE (*nodding towards the fire*): Log burst. (*Nods towards* ROSE.) Embers caught him full in face.

SOLDIER (*sarcastically*): Nasty.

ROSE (*turns*): I be fine now.

(*To* JANE:) Thank you for your comfort.

JANE (*patronisingly, to* SOLDIER): Don't fret yourself little man, I'll not dally further so if I'm late will be my jig roasting, not yours.

ROSE: Ride with care, sir.

JANE: I will that too, sir.

She turns and goes.

Silence.

SOLDIER (*making conversation*): Folly pure folly, is it not, leaving you and I alone. I thought orders was for others to return at dusk.

ROSE: Their orders was to return with spy dead or alive with preference to the latter state.

SOLDIER: Aye, well, by my reckoning commonsense should sometimes give leeway to orders.

Pause.

Or do you not agree?

ROSE: Aye.

SOLDIER (*moves closer*): I was apt to thinking you a bit queer but now I see I am mistaken, are you not the one fancying himself for having cuckolded the parson?

ROSE: I think not.

SOLDIER: Aye – is you – crowing in your sleep thrice 'Grace, Grace'.

ROSE: That be twice. Thrice is this number. (*She holds up three fingers.*)

SOLDIER: She be your sweetheart then? Is she? She is that, I can tell. What's she like then?

ROSE: You think this war will soon be over?

SOLDIER: You missing it that much then?

Pause.

Aye, by my reckoning we have the better of them, but war will not end for me whilst notion of Royalty still kicking. Is the thought of those wastrel bastards getting their true deserts keeps me going.

ROSE: Then you are n'ere beset by fear?

SOLDIER: Me? Nay.

Pause.

Why then, are you?

ROSE: Aye.

SOLDIER: Well, sometimes my gut do behave of its own accord like it was nothing to do with my head. But I think that be the same for most.

ROSE: I don't know.

Silence.

SOLDIER (*almost mumbled*): First time I did kill a man I did cast up. I had no notion of how bloody the mess would be.

ROSE: Did you never see death before?

SOLDIER: Aye, my sister died when I was but not five years old. But it was more like seeing a body asleep.

ROSE: And did you never see a woman swam?

SOLDIER: Oh aye, but that was more sport, she was a lewd-tongued old woman used to frighten me as a boy.

ROSE: You still look like a boy to me.

SOLDIER: By looks on you, you be even younger than I.

He moves closer.

God knows I've seen more hair on a woman.

ROSE *moves out of the light of the fire.*

Whilst we are about speaking the truth, I've never known a woman. I do pretend I have but I've not.

ROSE: Did you not know your mother?

SOLDIER (*scoffs*): Aye. Not by that meaning. (*He nudges* ROSE.) You know.

(*Then piteously:*) I suppose I might die not knowing.

Pause.

What's it like then?

Pause.

What's the game? I've all but laid my soul bare to you.

ROSE *gestures to him to be quiet. And points to a* LOYALIST SOLDIER, *standing, some way off, back to them and out of breath.*

(*Handing his pistol to* ROSE:) Have that cocked. (*Creeping up from behind he seizes the* LOYALIST.) Cam along with you, sir, where we can see you better. (*Dragging his victim in a stranglehold towards the fire.*) Now out with it, what is your business?

ROSE: He can't speak for your arm crushing his apple.

SOLDIER (*shoves his opponent, who is face up, to the ground*): And looks like a jerkin stuffed full of documents. Let's see what secrets we have in here.

He bends, puts his hand inside the jerkin and pulls it out again quickly.

It be a wench. (*Then with glee to* ROSE:) We have ourselves a wench here.

(*To the* WOMAN:) Aye and now I see your face, you be pretty in spite of your costume.

He kisses her roughly. She turns her head and spits in his face.

What sort of whore runs with Loyalist bastards eh? No need to answer on that for we're about to find out.

ROSE: No.

SOLDIER: Fair's fair, me first. (*Sitting on the* WOMAN. *He takes his sword off and throws it aside.*)

ROSE *remembering* GRACE'*s advice, lets out an unnerving howl of laughter.*

Don't take on, you'll get your turn. (*Then on seeing* ROSE *advance, pistol in hand.*) And it's not that gun you'll be needing, son. (*The* WOMAN *takes this moment to struggle from underneath him but he restrains her.*) Not so fast.

She scratches his face.

You little vixen.

They struggle on the ground in front of the fire. ROSE *realises that should she shoot, she might hit the wrong one. Putting the pistol down she goes to the fire and tearing a red hot branch, waits till the* SOLDIER *is on top of the* WOMAN *and puts it down his back. He screams and lets go. A shot is fired. And it is the woman,* BRIDGET, *who stands shaking, but her pistol pointed at* ROSE. *They stand in silence, the body of the* SOLDIER *between them.*

BRIDGET: So it was to be your turn next?

Pause.

ROSE: You will not make your way alive from here without my help.

BRIDGET: You must take me for a halfwit. I will not leave you here whilst you still have tongue in your head.

ROSE (*looks at the body*): I will ride with you.

BRIDGET: Aye. In front   this pointing to your back, and if I am brought down, I shan't be alone.

Scene Two

The church.
     HELEN'*s husband a* PARSON, *is sitting in the pulpit making notes.* HELEN *enters, pausing to give the inside of the font a wipe. She walks down the aisle towards the pulpit.*

HELEN: May I be granted words with you husband?

PARSON: Presently, dear. Not now for I am too busy.

HELEN: And what is this task?

She starts to step up in the pulpit.

PARSON: Woman are not allowed in the pulpit. Take thy foot off from that step.

HELEN *obeys*.

I am recording events in my diary.

HELEN: You don't need to do that perched up there.

PARSON: It serves to keep me ever mindful of my responsibility to my congregation.

HELEN: But you can't have anything to record other than 'today I wrote in my diary' for you've done nothing else.

PARSON (*impatiently*): I won't be a moment, I am just writing history.

HELEN (*wandering over to the lectern*): And where is the reason behind that?

PARSON: In many years hence men will want to read it and find out about the accounts and happenings of our time.

HELEN: You only know what goes on inside a church. Could I not help you with it?

PARSON: A woman cannot write, for even if she has a mind to understand the lines on paper, her emotions get in the way of truth.

Pointing to his diary.

This is plain statement of fact so it will not be questioned as to its accuracy in the future.

HELEN: What does it detail?

PARSON: You need not be troubled with it.

HELEN: I'm sure t'would improve under my guidance.

PARSON: Don't be foolish, women don't make history.

HELEN: Best read me your version before my curiosity causes me to test if the bird can fly.

Meaning the lectern, which is a wooden eagle.

PARSON (*sighs*): Very well. If it will mean some peace for me and be of some amusement to you.

HELEN (*mutters*): It will be of little else I'm sure.

PARSON (*reads as though delivering a sermon*): 'The war has rid us of many evils not least of the evil embodied in some of the female sex who were weighed in the balance and found wanting. Suitably dealt with through rigorous court procedures and brought to justice either swum or hung.'

HELEN (*curtly*): You've repeated the word evil twice.

PARSON (*casually*): T'is part of women's nature since life began with Eve.

HELEN: I have heard that so many times the words form wax and block my ears.

PARSON: God's word writ since time began. Is not for mortals to meddle with.

HELEN (*wild with rage, sweeps the bible from the lectern to the floor, smashes her fists on the lectern and jumping up and down shouting*): Why can't you change? Why can't you change?

An elderly WOMAN PARISHIONER *enters from the main door at the back, scurries to a back pew and kneels, hands tightly pressed together, eyes firmly shut. On seeing her, the* PARSON *scrambles from the pulpit, crosses to* HELEN.

PARSON (*in hushed whisper*): Do not take on in such a hysterical humour, calm yourself. Do you want for us to be footing another bill from the quack?

HELEN (*calmly*): Pray continue.

Simultaneously the PARISHIONER *starts to mumble a jumbled up, only half-remembered version of the Lord's Prayer.*

Our father witch chart in heaven
Hello to thy brain
Give us this day our daily bread
Forgive us our panes

As we forgive those will be done
Thy kindom be done
As now or never
Lead us up to temptation
Deliver us from weevil
Thine be the glory every lasting son
For ever and ever, Amen.

*The words cannot be heard clearly,
i.e. it should not compete with the
following dialogue, but should
continue until HELEN speaks
directly to her.*

PARSON: This is but a humble
clergyman's account.

HELEN (*nods*): Aye. (*She waits, tapping
her foot.*)

PARSON (*scrambling with his notes;
reads in hushed tone*): Some of these
women were unfortunate. (*Looks up.*)
See, I too can find sympathy.
(*Continues reading.*) In fact many
were merely harmless, repulsive,
foul-smelling hags who cursed every-
one who cam near and were quite mad
in the head.

HELEN (*aggressively*): Can you not know
what a dangerous thing you write.

PARSON: You are rapidly putting me in
bad humour. Now I have quite lost the
flow, please content yourself to leave
me be.

HELEN (*coldly*): Presently, dear, for I
wanted to speak with you.

PARSON: Well, speak then and leave me
in peace.

HELEN (*calmly*): Have no fear. Firstly,
are you a Quaker?

PARSON: In our Lord's name what
blasphemy are you asking of me?
You know my religion. Steady as the
rock of St Peter.

HELEN: Even he was known to quake in
a cock's presence.

PARSON: Do not play games with the
scriptures.

HELEN: Well, I am a Quaker.

PARSON: You cannot be, you are wed
to me.

HELEN (*serenely*): Oh dear. Now a
Quaker must be married to another
Quaker.

PARSON: Have you been victim to
bites from mad dog?

HELEN: I must make sure. You say you
are not a Quaker?

PARSON: You know I'm not.

HELEN: Then I cannot stay married to
you.

PARSON: Have you lost all sense?

HELEN: No. The dilemma is solved. I
wilt leave you to your solitude now
husband. Thank you for sparing me
the time.

*She turns on her heel and strides down
the aisle.*

PARSON: But you can't.

HELEN (*on reaching the praying
PARISHIONER, stops briefly and taps
her on the head*): That pes would be
put to better use saving your knees
whilst scrubbing floors. Take it with
you.

She continues walking.

PARSON (*trying to catch up with his
wife whilst retaining his dignity*):
Helen? (*On reaching the
PARISHIONER he lays his hand on
her head so she sinks back to her
knees.*) Bless you, child.

(*Continues to follow HELEN.*) But
you are my wife.

*Pausing only to spit in the font,
HELEN goes, shutting the door behind
her. Once outside she laughs.*

Scene Three

A rowing boat on the river.
  *ROSE and BRIDGET are seated
opposite each other in a small rowing
boat. ROSE sits back trailing her burnt*

hand in the water. BRIDGET *rows but cannot take her eyes off* ROSE *which proves a preferable pastime to rowing.*

ROSE (*sitting up*): Shall I take my turn now?

BRIDGET: Your hand is too sore. Besides I am far from tired.

ROSE: What ails you then?

BRIDGET (*blurts out*): I thought I must be only one of my kind under the sky, and now I have found you — is that joy which distracts me.

ROSE (*laughs*): Will be short-lived if it prevents you from pulling on the oars — for we shall perish.

BRIDGET: I am too happy. I care not.

ROSE: Well I do. Here. Stand up and change places.

They both stand. The boat rocks. ROSE, *holds onto* BRIDGET *to steady herself.* BRIDGET *kisses* ROSE. *Both slightly surprised and shocked and sit down again without having changed places.*

BRIDGET: Rose, cam home with me.

ROSE: Home?

BRIDGET (*starting to row with renewed vigour*): You'd not want for anything again.

ROSE: You must have wanted for something — to leave its comfort.

BRIDGET: Was for something I didn't want, namely a rich toad with his brain in his stones and one thought between them.

ROSE: And if he still waits for you? Your mother will put me to work in her garden no doubt.

BRIDGET: She'll be only too over-whelmed with joy to see me alive and that you have no money will play no part when I tell you saved my life. Rose, you will have riches and servants such as you never imagined.

ROSE: And do you imagine that this war

with its blood and death and gore has meant nothing to me? For it is about no one being a servant to another. No more rich and idle by virtue of their birth but every person equal.

BRIDGET: Every man. For they might each have equality but they still take upon themselves, rich or poor, a wife who is but a slave and not paid into the bargain.

ROSE: But now it is you who talk of servants. I am a servant. Do you think I'd take it upon myself to treat my kind likewise.

Pause.

BRIDGET: Then I shall share with you all I have.

ROSE: Then cam back with me?

BRIDGET: Back where?

ROSE: To my village.

BRIDGET (*shakes her head*): I'd be out of place.

ROSE: I'd not be out of place with your kind?

BRIDGET: Money can buy a person any place.

ROSE (*ironically*): Oh Aye. Money.

BRIDGET: Please think on it Rose.

ROSE (*shakes her head*): My longing to see my friends again be too strong.

BRIDGET: They will be asleep now.

ROSE: But the morning will unite us.

Pause.

BRIDGET: Then spend this night with me.

Scene Four

A misty day by the pond.
Enter ROSE, *on foot. She can just about see* HELEN *standing on a tree stump and* MARY, ANN *and an unknown* WOMAN *standing motionless beside* HELEN.

ROSE (*approaching slowly*): So none have mislaid our pledge.

HELEN (*shouts*): Cam closer, sir, show yourself.

ROSE *moves closer and finds the only person there is* HELEN.

ROSE (*to herself*): Two years and I'd quite forgot tricks marsh mist could play.

HELEN: You be a stranger here?

ROSE: No more stranger than you, Helen.

HELEN: Who are you? (*She takes two steps towards* ROSE.) Rose? Young Rose?

She hugs her.

ROSE (*laughs and frees herself*): Steady, lest the village tongues have us tied in holy state afore we can be acquainted again.

HELEN (*stands back*): My, what a handsome fellow you make. I hope two years at war has not turned you to the habits of other young men.

ROSE (*quietly*): I am home.

HELEN: Rose. Oh Rose, I am pleased to see this day. What have you done to your hand?

ROSE (*putting her hand behind her back*): Nothing. And how have you fared these two years since?

HELEN: You have been constant in my thoughts, Rose, not least because you were right. My dealings with doctors served only to punish and humiliate me. I do swear they loathe us worse than the rest of their kind. But, for me now that is finished.
(*Carefully*:) And what news of Jane?

ROSE: I know not where she is. So make cheerful with your tales for there must be some event you can recall which will warm my heart.

HELEN: Rose . . .

ROSE: Helen, tell me only of cheerful things. Tell me of London and the jick-a-joy women kicked up there.

HELEN: Oh aye, and why would you be interested in peace protests when you was making money in the war?

ROSE: Oh rouse yourself.

HELEN: Was all but wonderful, Rose, how we wished you'd seen it.

Slight pause.

Mary. (*She falters but continues.*) becam so carried away with her protesting against violence that she broke the Duke of Richmond's staff over his own head.

ROSE (*laughs*): That do sound like her.

HELEN: That is not but half of it. The chant went up over and over 'We will not be wives and tie up our lives to villainous slavery'.

ROSE: So another war broke out at the moment I'll wager.

HELEN: The retort was varied but in the usual manner. From contemptible vileness to what they deemed as reasoned arguments like 'Go home and wash your plates'. But you have never heard women's voice so strong. One immediately rejoined 'You give us something to put on our plates and then we'll wash 'em'. While another cried 'We ent washing no more plates for you'. And another much to Ann and Mary's delight screamed 'When I have your head on a plate then I'll wash it off'. I had to keep reminding the other two that our purpose there was to ask for peace. And we met there women and, Rose, they had so many ideas like yourself you'd have talked till your clacker fell apart. Cam home with me so we can eat and talk at leisure. Is too cold standing on this spot.

ROSE: But first you must reveal to me, what are these clothes you have on?

HELEN: I have become a Quaker.

ROSE (*alarmed*): You mean thou has the shaking pox? I thought you looked in peculiar shape tossing your arms on this stump.

HELEN (*laughs*): It is but the new religion.

ROSE (*more alarmed*): That is good news? The misery religion has wrought us. Helen, what folly is this?

HELEN: Afore you lambast me hear me out for in this new religion I am a preacher.

ROSE: You?

HELEN: Any person who feels so moved can be.

ROSE: No doubt St Paul's corpse be a-quaking too.

HELEN: I'll have you know I can draw quite a crowd with details of my visions which I can reveal to you are well structured so as to be precise on pointing out the nature of women's accumbrements.

ROSE: But what of your husband? I perceive your walls would crumble under strain of two preachers practising their sermons within.

HELEN (*gleefully*): The way of this new religion be if your spouse be not of the same persuasion you can leave for another who shares your beliefs.

ROSE: Is far less of an evil solution that ridding yourself of a wife by getting her hung.

Pause. HELEN does not respond.

So you have some bad news? You have taken yourself a Shaker husband?

HELEN (*smiles*): My visions are such that I cannot seem to find a suitable one. You wait, we shall stir up this country in this time of unrest till woman shall laugh till she cries at very notion of being pinned down to man.

ROSE: I will fetch the others and we shall have a meeting like never afore.

HELEN: No. (*Gently:*) Rose, you can't.

ROSE (*ruefully*): Oh, waste no worry over me. Dressed as a man has given me wonderful freedom to go charging about where I want.

HELEN: Let's sit down.

ROSE: For why? We're not in church. (*Pause. So she sits on the tree stump.*) Right, I am sat down. Oh, Mary and Ann are still in London?

HELEN (*sits down next to her and holds her hand*): Rose, Ann and Mary are dead.

ROSE: Dead? They are dead?

HELEN: Yes. Hung.

ROSE (*in disbelief*): Hung? For what?

HELEN: For what else?

ROSE: We did rid this place of the pricker, did we not? I can't believe it. Did we not rid this place . . .?

HELEN (*gently*): About the same time as we went our separate ways he returned with fame, fortune and self-appointed title and powers and set about his task more zealously than ever.

ROSE: But you said you all went to London.

HELEN: Aye but others returned for child, whilst I stayed on to waste money on their doctors.

ROSE (*letting go of HELEN's hand, stands and turns accusingly, raising her voice*): They are dead? And you are content to sit here holding my hand and say they are dead and you did nothing?

HELEN (*stands, angrily, almost shouting*): And what would you know of what's been done? There has been one hundred hung since you've been gone and to my reckoning double that number swam and drowned unrecorded. And you demand of me what has been done when women live in fear of drawing next breath for it bringing the noose closer to their windpipe. When women take to practising holding their breath in hope they might sink and be then dragged from the water alive.

(*Quieter*:) And you ask me what has been done in this place where we dare not even look at one another or, God forbid, converse for that be deemed conspiracy enough. And you will tell me the old story that love is as strong as death? For in these times, to my mind, life all but holds a weak flame to fear.

ROSE (*sits ashamed*): I did not know.

HELEN (*calmly but still angry*): And well might you brag of men's clothes. For it does not pay to be a daughter today. The child, aye, with nor two years of life behind her was swam along with her mother for the crime — the crime of being descendant of Eve — which be but a mispelling of Evil to their minds. (*Sadly*:) Rose, they have all but bled our village dry of our sex.

ROSE: I dare but ask the question burning in my head.

HELEN: We know what they can do. We have paid for that knowledge at such cost that those remaining can no longer afford to be left divided.

ROSE: And Grace? Helen, what of Grace?

HELEN (*gently*): Rose, I know not whether she is yet living or has died from her sufferings.

ROSE: She is in gaol?

HELEN: Would be to no avail, Rose. T'is too well kept and her brain is worse scrambled than a broke egg.

ROSE: She is in town gaol?

HELEN (*sighs*): Aye. Where hangings are public sport. As the crowd never knows the victim, not a shadow passes through their eyes.

HELEN *goes off*.

ROSE (*sings*):

Rosie's Song

When I was fighting alongside the men
For the freedom they had taken by right,
I wondered if I'd visit my village again
And return to another dear fight.
The price I have paid to walk as a man
Has lost me the trust of my kind
And it had been part of a much bigger plan
But now I am back here I find —

I fought in their wars, and not with my sister,
My pay is in shillings and being called mister,
While women have hanged and drowned all the time,
And being a woman's a death-bringing crime.
I gave up my woman in wearing a disguise,
Partly by bribery, partly by lies,
And what they have got is a soldier to fight
And one woman less to defend her birthright.

The freedom to pass as a man is a curse —
No woman would choose that for her life —
And marriage to men is no better or worse
For bearing the name of a wife.
The only way through is to stand out and strong,
And not wear disguise in *their* fight,
But to be with the women here where I belong
And to call on our strength and our might.

I fought in their wars, and not with my sister,
My pay is in shillings and being called mister
While women have hanged and drowned all the time
And being a woman's a death-bringing crime.
I gave up my woman in wearing a disguise

Partly by bribery, partly by lies,
And what they have got is a soldier to
    fight
And one less woman to defend her
    birthright.

For they take the skills and the powers
    that we share
With women who trust in our healing.
For they cut and thrust, and no one
    will spare
So no woman dare speak what she's
    feeling.
But I shall take power and we'll start a
    war
Against doctors and soldiers and men
Who challenge our right and seize at
    the core
Of our birthright, our freedom. Fight
    again!

Scene Five

The gaol.
    *A very unpleasant gaol with an equally
unpleasant-looking GAOLER. ROSE
approaches him, placing a flask of beer
on the table. Although she is still dressed
as a man she is no longer dressed as a
soldier.*

GAOLER: And what's a young
    gentleman like yourself be wanting
    with me (*Sarcastically*.), sir?

ROSE: I'm a visitor to these parts and
    enquiring as to when the next hanging
    might be?

GAOLER: Luck's out, sir. Was this very
    morning two pretty young things
    drew a great crowd. You'll be cursing
    yourself if you missed it.

ROSE: So you'll be keeping an empty
    gaol, then, sir?

GAOLER: Not in their interest nor mine,
    if gaol was empty I'd not have work.
    Like days of cock fighting. No good if
    you finished off your last cock. Rest
    assured no shortages of women round
    here, dare say we'll have more in by
    the end of the week.

ROSE: Is an old woman I'm after.

GAOLER (*firmly*): Now listen here,
    young sir. There's still plenty of young
    maids out there what would be happy
    to service a young man like yourself.
    I don't know what you gents think I'm
    running here.

ROSE (*abruptly*): I do not want that
    (*Spitting out the word*:), sir.

GAOLER: You don't look the sort,
    granted, but you can never tell, I am
    afraid to say. Some of them Puritans
    are the worse.

ROSE: You don't understand.

GAOLER (*mockingly*): Aye. I dare say.

ROSE: I do not want her for any purpose
    other than talking.

GAOLER (*seriously*): Forgive me, sir, I
    now understand. She put a curse on
    your family and you want one last
    chance to remove it, lest further
    tragedy strike.

ROSE: Aye, aye, that's right.

GAOLER: Well, out of luck again. That
    old hag wouldn't know if she was
    saying the Lord's Prayer or cursing
    a cow. Her brain's curdled worse than
    the milk she's bewitched.

ROSE: Has she been here long?

GAOLER: Some months now. Aye,
    they're hoping for a bit more life outta
    her. Now that's an arse-about-face idea
    if ever I heard one. Still these days
    crowd gets mighty despondent if them
    what's hanged be a corpse afore
    hangman even gets started.

ROSE: Take me to her.

GAOLER: Now hold still, young sir.

ROSE: Give me a cup of that and keep
    rest. (*She takes a cup of beer.*)

GAOLER: Through there and mind you
    leave her in the same state you found
    her in.

    ROSE *finds* GRACE *chained at the
feet and whispers for fear of being
overheard by the* GAOLER.

ROSE: Grace? (*Gently trying to rouse her:*) Grace? Grace? Is me.

GRACE (*mumbles*): Oh another imp, a rat this time. Our father who art in heaven hallowed be thy name the divel. I have more imps than stars in the sky and they all seem to sleep here in my bed with me so fly and take them with you.

ROSE: Grace?

GRACE: Young man, I am done, done with thee all.

ROSE *gently tilts the cup to* GRACE's *mouth.*

GRACE (*spits it back in* ROSE's *face*): Every woman has her breaking point and you have seen mine thrice over. Leave me be.

ROSE *doesn't know what to do or say. Impulsively she undoes her outer garment and takes* GRACE's *hand, placing it between her vest and outer garment, on her breast.*

ROSE: Grace, it's me.

GRACE (*looks into* ROSE's *face trying to recall who it belongs to. At last she says faintly*): Rose?

ROSE: None other.

GRACE: I knew you'd came. (*Her hand falls and she slips into half-consciousness.*)

GAOLER (*shouts*): Shift your parliament, sir. You don't know what you'll catch in there.

ROSE (*returns to the* GAOLER): I trust the ale is to your liking.

GAOLER: Not so much as to grant any further favours.

ROSE: And how would they know? If she died?

GAOLER: I've got a tongue in my head, ain't I?

ROSE: And they'd have to see the body?

GAOLER: You think stink's not bad enough when they're alive. I get the corpses shifted quick enough. Just get a doctor or a priest to sign paper.

ROSE: I would like to take her.

GAOLER: You're a strange one, you are, but I have no time for this riddle.

ROSE: And for you to tell them she died.

GAOLER: You would eh? Just like that I'd let a young gent whose tastes are out of course make off with a dying hag.

ROSE: How much? (*She drops a coin on the table.*)

GAOLER: It's more than my job's worth.

ROSE (*drops another coin in front of him*): And what's your job worth?

GAOLER (*flatly*): More than that.

ROSE *puts another coin down.*

Who'd sign the paper?

ROSE: I would.

GAOLER (*unsure*): Oh, aye.

ROSE: I'm a doctor. (*She puts another coin down.*)

GAOLER: A doctor you say now? And what would a doctor be wanting of a half-witted crone with one foot in hell and the other on piss-soaked straw?

ROSE: Bodies are valuable to our science.

GAOLER: Aye, I have heard something of the like.

ROSE: So you'll do it?

GAOLER: Not for four shillings I won't.

ROSE: Five shillings. No more.

GAOLER: If you're caught I know nothing of this.

ROSE: Very well. Take her cramp rings off.

GAOLER (*throwing* ROSE *the keys*): Take 'em off yourself.

ROSE *returns to* GRACE *and undoes the chains.*

ROSE: You're as good as home, Grace.

A hand darts out from under the straw and grabs ROSE's *ankle.* ROSE *visibly jumps but keeps herself from crying out. The hand belongs to another prisoner who had completely hidden herself in the straw on* ROSE's *arrival. Now* ROSE *can see the hand belongs to a young woman –* URSULA.

URSULA *holds* ROSE's *arm and* GRACE's *hand.*

Who are you?

Pause.

For why am I asking when I know you are a young woman waiting to be hung.

She pulls herself free from URSULA's *grasp and returns to the* GAOLER.

GAOLER: Give over them keys and sign here.

ROSE: How much d'ye want for the girl?

GAOLER: Cam te yer sense then, sir, seen the prettier one. Now she's worth a lot more, that one, she is. You won't get no nagging out of her neither. Divel took her ears and tongue.

ROSE (*shouts*): What do you want for her?

GAOLER: You must be a young man of some wealth, your voice not yet broke neither, there's a thing.

ROSE (*calmer*): Two.

GAOLER: Don't mock me.

ROSE: Take it or leave it.

GAOLER: Too risky them both dying together as it were. Too suspicious.

ROSE (*snaps*): The plague didn't look suspicious, did it?

GAOLER: Your lot making money outta it did though. Three.

ROSE: Three. (*She gives him the money.*)

GAOLER: Ooh, make a hard bargain you do, sir. Best keep to your part and sign papers here for me.

ROSE (*does so*): If all the wrongs men had done to them were counted up and laid on doorsteps of where they came. Not a man left in the land who not be quaking.

GAOLER: Ah, now that do go a long way to explain your oddity, sir. You be one of them new religious lot.

Scene Six

GRACE's *house.*
   ROSE *is trying, with little success, to get* GRACE *to eat some broth.* URSULA *sits in the corner. There is a knock on the door.*
   ROSE *opens the door to a young* DOCTOR.

DOCTOR: You sent word for me?

ROSE: Aye and money too.

DOCTOR: I'll do my best for you, sir, on that you may depend. Well, let's go take a look, shall we?

ROSE: She is afore your eyes. (*Nodding towards* GRACE.)

DOCTOR: My mistake, young gentleman. I am used to tending livestock first and then asked to see to the wife. What t'is the rhyme you farm people have – 'If the cow kicks off, mighty cross, if the wife kicks off, no big loss.'

ROSE: I am no farmer, sir. So it be a notion you'd do well to disabuse yourself of.

DOCTOR: So it is your wife first and foremost.

ROSE: No, not her. But her mother. (*Chronologically this would be doubtful so she corrects herself:*) Her mother's mother.

DOCTOR: You have paid me good money, sir, but in truth she is really too old to bother with.

ROSE: Not to me.

DOCTOR: She is weak and frail.

ROSE: That is plain enough. I don't have to part with payment for looking through my own eyes. She does talk nonsense, such words as she speaks come forth all jumbled.

DOCTOR: She has a fever. (*He opens his bag and produces a knife and* URSULA *starts screaming.*)

ROSE: Can you put the knife away, sir.

DOCTOR: If she is to be cured I am to bleed her and let the badness drain out.

ROSE (*gestures to* URSULA *to be quiet*): Please leave off that noise. I will see no harm comes to her.

DOCTOR: T'is your wife who needs attention, sir.

ROSE (*referring to* GRACE): Have you none of nature's remedies for this sickness, sir?

DOCTOR: I took you for an intelligent man, sir, and far advanced from the rubbish spouted by old crones. If I am to save your wife's mother's mother I am to cut her. (*He advances on* GRACE.)

GRACE (*barely whispers*): No.

ROSE: That is your answer.

DOCTOR: But you claim she knows not what she says.

ROSE: Her life's blood's not bad, it doesn't warrant flowing away. Leave her be.

DOCTOR: I have come all this way and as yet administered to no one. Shall I take a look at your wife?

URSULA *starts to scream again.*

ROSE: No. No, cam away. You only seem to aggravate her condition.

DOCTOR: Now you and I know, sir, women are bad let down with nerves. There are several cures for that.

ROSE: She has suffered, sir. Is natural to have nerves.

DOCTOR: But can you not see? Is but your unyielding obstinacy that hampers our work. Forward thinkers term us saviours of mankind, Our science is the new hope. Only thing your cure depends on is your trust in it.

ROSE: Take more than that to convince me that the knife is cure for anything, never mind everything.

DOCTOR: It is within my power to right the ills plaguing both these females and your belief in me will cause you to be grateful for the service I am about to perform. (*He shrugs.*) Most likely their faith in the old hocus-pocus herb medicine that has landed them in this state of ill-health.

ROSE: Aye. Most probably was, though not in the way you're meaning. Thank you for your trouble, door is behind you.

DOCTOR (*scoffs*): Natural remedies. (*He takes out a knife.*) This won't hurt.

ROSE (*drawing out her sword*): Is there something amiss about your lugs or would you like me to perform on you your own style of cure and in the mark of St Peter?

DOCTOR: T'is not my usual reception. Many are overcome with gratitude to see me.

ROSE: I'll not be overcome with gratitude until you step other side of the door.

DOCTOR: I would just like to say . . .

ROSE *advances, sword in hand. The* DOCTOR's *knife looking quite pathetic by comparison, causing him to make for the door.*

ROSE: Sling thy hook.

DOCTOR (*with as much dignity as possible*): Goodnight.

He goes.

ROSE: Cut the badness out? With their judgement, soon enough there'd be none left of us. (*To* URSULA:) Do you have any idea what would make her well?

URSULA *turns away.*

Oh, what have they done to us? What have they done? (*She turns away and cries.*)

Pause.

URSULA *turns, shocked and confused by* ROSE's *tears as she thinks she is a man. Gently she approaches her.* ROSE *looks up.*

URSULA (*confirming*): I am free.

URSULA *takes* ROSE's *now festering hand, and holds it open.* ROSE *pulls back.* URSULA *waits.* ROSE *holds it out again.* URSULA *cleans her hand, places Calendula leaves on the sore and bandages it.*

ROSE: Thank you.

URSULA *takes the water over to* GRACE *and starts to bathe her hands and face, then rolls up the sleeves of* GRACE's *garments. Realising that* ROSE *(a man) is watching, she turns* ROSE *round so she faces the door and has her back turned to* GRACE. *Enter* LADY H. URSULA, *unaware of her entrance, continues with her task.*

LADY H: Oh, I was given to understand an old woman lived here.

ROSE: She is not fit to receive visitors.

LADY H: Is it not customary for a gentleman to bow when a lady enters his abode?

ROSE: Is it not customary for a lady to knock when she enters a gentleman's abode?

LADY H: Who are you?

ROSE: Never you mind. Please state your business here.

LADY H: You are a bold fellow. Be this your wife, timid from your tyranny?

ROSE: No, this be my sister.

LADY H: My, this is a rum household.

(*To* URSULA:) How would you like to cam and work for me, girl? T'is utterly tiresome, most of my staff have kicked off or been knocked off. There's not a bod willing to take care of my babes for love nor money.

Silence.

You'd do well to answer me.

URSULA *does not turn round.*

ROSE (*mockingly*): Forgive me. I was but musing on our language. Where the words 'for love' mean 'for nothing'.

LADY H: I cannot tell which is most addled, your mind or your mouth. No matter, I am not here to solve the riddle for you. And t'was not you to whom I was addressing myself in first place.

ROSE: If your household is so depleted you'd have been better preventing the deaths of those who so inconveniently got knocked off.

LADY H: Simple folk full of superstition and nonsense. And for certain not my place to interfere in their squabbles or rituals.

ROSE: Then is not your place to put your nose in this dwelling.

LADY H: It was the old woman's help I sought.

ROSE: Where were you when she needed help? She's too ill even to speak.

LADY H: A great pity, for these times are harsh set against my sex.

ROSE: If you feel them harsh, lady, may the divel take the rest of us.

LADY H: I have cam to accept that men have no understanding of bonds of accumberment between rich and poor amongst our sex.

ROSE: I will lend you half an ear.

LADY H (*gently*): My sister died in childbirth last week and babe was torn limb from limb in the name of their science with these barbarous instruments. (*She throws down two evil-looking hooks.*) There, that is their substitute for the midwife's hands of flesh.

ROSE: And you have borrowed them?

LADY H (*back to her old self*): Aye. If only to dispose of them. He will not use them further. After he committed foul deed I whopped him one over the skull with a poker, such was my temperament. T'was a blow from which he didn't recover.

ROSE: You killed him?

LADY H: Doesn't the good book say an eye for an eye, and a tooth for a tooth? Should be made to think afore he wields his authority in such a murderous manner.

ROSE (*despite herself is beginning to admire* LADY H): But you could be hung?

LADY H: These doctors can't find their way round a woman's body never mind a village on the marshes. Will be no shock to anyone that he disappeared.

ROSE: I hope it is not that you have cam to set the blame at this door.

LADY H: My sole purpose was to talk to the old woman and get these evil ways stopped before there is neither mother or babe left in the land.

ROSE: If Grace becomes well I shall be sure to tell her.

LADY H: Aye and to ask her advice about setting up schools for midwives. For rumour has it that one man has instrument which is true aid for difficult births such as were cause of anxiety to best-experienced midwives. But such is the nature of these bastards' code of conduct that he will only pass secret of it on to his son for no one has offered a high enough price. Ha, he has not bargained for what I will offer him, should I track his whereabouts down.

ROSE: I wish thee luck.

LADY H: Now I am off to hear that Quaker lady speak for I am half-way committed already. But if I might be permitted to make one last observation — it would be to note your sister's rudeness for she has not so much as acknowledged my presence.

ROSE: She is unaware of your presence for she cannot hear.

LADY H: Oh then I must make my case to her face. (*She taps* URSULA *on the shoulder.* URSULA *jumps with surprise.*)

ROSE: No

LADY H (*to* ROSE): You must allow your sister to do as she pleases. We have noted too much the desires of your sex and it has not served your health. (*To* URSULA:) How would you like to work for me child?

URSULA (*not understanding, looks at* ROSE *and signs*): What she say?

ROSE: Bear her no mind (*Using dismissive arm-waving gestures.*) Nothing. Nothing.

LADY H (*to* ROSE): Let her choose for herself. (*Saying and miming to* URSULA:) You want to work for me? Sewing, cooking, cleaning, looking after my children? For money.

URSULA *nods enthusiastically then looks at* GRACE *and then back at* LADY H.

(LADY H *nods.*) Aye. You may continue to nurse the sick woman also.

ROSE: She does not want to work for you.

LADY H: Seems you are mistaken.

GRACE (*whispers*): Rose. Rose.

ROSE (*goes to* GRACE): Grace?

GRACE: I knew you'd cam.

LADY H (*sighs*): Be of no use, sir. Her mind still tricks her mouth.

Enter the DOCTOR. *The* DOCTOR *and* LADY H *sing.*

From a Dish to a Dish

DOCTOR (*sings*):
We're here to stay, no more witches and midwives
With potions and herbs and wasting of lives.
We're gaining control and refining our tools
Creating a science, replacing these fools.

LADY H (*sings*):
Three centuries ago they started with hooks,
But the medicine man will next control our looks —
For they have moved on from bleeding out our life
To creating the next generation of perfect wife.

DOCTOR (*sings*):
Fertilised in a Petri dish as a result of egg donation,
Transplanted by the doctor, father of the future, perfect nation,
Completed the laparoscopy, done with amniocentesis,
Will abort if results show a less than first-rate foetus.

Have mastered techniques of *in vitro* fertilisation,
Surrogacy, ectogenesis and super-ovulation,
Won't stop now, intrauterine surgery will enrich our lives,
And cloning will ensure that males outnumber wives.

For women's dispensability will not hamper surgery,
Experiments will never end the bank of frozen embryos
We divided at the 4-cell stage
For chromosome analysis and sex preselection.

We don't admit that no one knows
The results of trans-species fertilisation.

And hormonal manipulation is bombing women's ovaries
And it's unethical not to experiment on spare embryos.
We're in charge of the future, the future perfect nation,
We're in charge of women's bodies, and isn't she a sensation.

I look at her in the Petri dish
And I fuck her with scientists' wish
That I'll create a full-grown dish
Who'll satisfy my every wish
And I'll father the perfect nation.

LADY H (*sings*):
From witches and midwives, they raped us with hooks,
Created their science, wrote us out of their books,
And now they're in charge of more than our looks —
Our future's in the hands of their reproductive technology.
And there's more at stake now than the right to children and gynaecology.

Scene Seven

The inn.
HELEN *stands on an upright barrel,* LADY H *next to her. Several women crowd round. The* PUBLICAN, *relieved that the bar separates him, fidgets nervously.*

HELEN: I speak not of Holy Ghost.

WOMAN 1: Thank God for that.

HELEN: Nor spooks or superstition, nor the fear of the immortal or invisible but of those who have taken it upon themselves to think they are the God-only-wise.

WOMAN 1: Who?

HELEN: The wreckers of earthly beauty and nature herself.

WOMAN 2 (*to* WOMAN 1): Oh men.

WOMAN 1: Oh aye, if my husband had another brain it would be lonely.

HELEN: The battle of men against men is not the war of our time but the fight women have had for their lives. We have shaken their opinion of us as the weaker sex . . .

WOMAN 3: Weaker sex ho ho.

HELEN: And they have responded with ways more forceful than ever before. Now is not the time for slowing down, for our lives swing more lightly in the balance than ever before.

PUBLICAN: Now then 'mistress', I'm sure your husbands must be fretting as to where you are. And fretting all the more I dare say if they knew.

WOMAN 1: If you know what's best for you, you'll keep your jaws still.

HELEN (*continues*): Women will flee for the lives of their unborn children from the spittle-house rather than endure birthing at the mercy of the doctors' tools. The disease that follows will be worse than any plague yet known, except it remain unchartered for t'is our sex alone again that will suffer and die from it.

LADY H: Listen to her, she speaks absolute truth

WOMAN 2 (*to* WOMAN 3): If Lady Horse-face has got herself here, is not for the likes of us. Let's make off.

PUBLICAN: That's right dear, you do that, you're frightening off my customers.

They all turn and stare at him.

WOMAN 1: Sit down.

PUBLICAN: Aye. Maybe I need a rest.

WOMAN 3: Certainly your mouth does.

The PUBLICAN *sits, disappearing from view.*

LADY H: I have a pamphlet here, written by two women and I'd like to read . . .

WOMAN 2: Do we want a reading from her?

WOMAN 3: Let her speak, for is not writ by her and how else can we learn of its contents?

WOMAN 1: Who was it writ by then?

LADY H: They couldn't use their own names for front page but ones they chose were better than any family name in the land. 'Mary Tattlewell' and 'Joane Hit-him-home Spinster'.

PUBLICAN *puts his face above the bar.*

WOMAN 2: How does 'Ann Hit-him-over-the-brain-pan-with-a-tankard' sound?

The PUBLICAN *promply disappears from view.*

WOMAN 3: Tell us what they have to say then.

LADY H: If women were ever allowed to be taught singing and dancing t'was only to please men's licentious appetites. That women are taught nothing than to get a husband and what life could a woman ever expect if marriage was the be all and end all of existence. At same time they cite how female character is preferable to the male.

WOMAN 2: What did you do when we was begging and them refused was cursing?

WOMAN (*to* WOMAN 2): She didn't so much as lift a chicken leg off her table, that's what she did.

HELEN: The hanging and butchering of women is part of the same hatred. We must make certain that we be the last generation to bear witness to the wrongs done to us in name of science. That our daughter's daughter and her daughter too will know what we know.

WOMAN 3: She is right and t'is not only labourers' daughters what need telling. I say Lady H should join us.

LADY H: We will be despised, ridiculed and deemed mad but I vouchsafe that I am prepared to forgo my privilege in the name of truth.

WOMAN 1: Aye let her be part of us for we can no longer do nothing but pray.

WOMAN 2: And not rest until we have won back our bodies for ourselves.

Scene Eight

GRACE's *home.*
Physically weak but mentally alert, GRACE *is reading* ROSE's *play.* ROSE *paces the floor.*

GRACE (*puts down the play having finished*): Rose, this is more than reward enough for teaching you to write.

ROSE: What did you like best? I saw you grinning like your mouth would crack.

GRACE: A fine story Rose. Aye and funny.

ROSE: Perhaps the best thing you have read by one of our sex?

GRACE: Rose, it is the only thing. But that makes it no less wonderful.

ROSE: Talk to me more about it, Grace.

GRACE: Presently. First, while it is just you and I, I want to tell you to take it on yourself to let Ursula know who you are. Well, you don't have to tell her you write plays but the least you can say is you're no man.

ROSE: I'll think on it. Now what did you think of your character?

GRACE: No you will not think on it, you'll do it. It's not fair to abuse her trust in this way.

ROSE: Trust, ha, took her time enough to reveal to me her understanding of healing.

GRACE (*coldly angry*): Rose, she saw her own mother hung for her pains. Do you think she'd want any part of that knowledge?

ROSE (*sulkily*): Then she went to work for Lady H.

GRACE (*abruptly*): Aye and have you not stopped to wonder on why? For why would a man buy her? She is working to repay the debt. And is for you to tell her money was hers by right. (*Then with warmth:*) And what of Jane — when she breezes in her confusion will know no bounds and trick even I into believing my mind is blown away again.

ROSE (*quietly*): Grace, I know not if she is still living.

GRACE (*gently*): You would know if she were dead.

ROSE: I never felt Mary and Ann were anything but alive.

GRACE: You knew when death had all but closed in on me.

ROSE: I had but one dream, Grace. Only that.

GRACE: But, I knew you'd cam.

ROSE: Several events cam between you and the dream. I do not now want to dwell on Jane for all manner of ills my running off may have caused her.

GRACE: Cam, that one could talk herself into the King's privy and out again. There are enough causes of death in war besides yourself. So you'd well not to beset yourself with guilt.

ROSE: Supposing?

Pause.

Oh let us talk about my play.

GRACE: Aye. Well, I have several recommendations that may improve it.

ROSE (*defensively*): What is wrong with it?

GRACE: Don't take on like a child. Is not in the writing, Rose. Though story is apt, like its mistress, to wander. But the ideas.

ROSE: Like what?

GRACE: If you keep interrupting I

cannot collect my thoughts. Firstly I am very proud of my part. Is a very generous picture you paint of me but you give impression that I was able to cure all manner of ills which is more like the story of son of God than me.

ROSE: But . . .

GRACE: I wasn't able, nor am I still. True I have perfected the use of some herbs and given some advice but I have no power over life and death. Your portrait of cunning women is too glowing for truth. So many have been killed in this purge who didn't know a sprig of dill from a cauliflower. They was chosen because they were women not because they were special. When we have received foul attentions from lord and from farmhand alike, t'is because we are women. It's a danger to claim it is because we are different in some way.

ROSE: Who did they start on first, old women, cunning women, women alone, Mary and Ann. They were independent and did not carry on as men wished them to.

GRACE: But it didn't stop there, did it?

ROSE: No.

GRACE: Our sex with its single power to give birth, pose a threat to men's power over whole order of villages, towns, counties and countries. That control depends on women cur-tailing to men's ideals of how they should behave.

ROSE: So, if it is fact you want from me, happen there was women enough to cause trouble against each other.

GRACE: Because not only are men set against the woman named wicked but also the women and children whose livelihood depends on the approval of men.

ROSE: So the condemned woman is special. She has freed herself as much as is possible and will not keep her mouth still about it.

GRACE: What I am saying is that the tests and methods by which they decide who is evil are without two solutions. They are designed only to condemn. When they look for a witch they are looking for a woman and do not mistake thyself, any one of us will do.

ROSE (*impatiently*): Is a story, Grace, not a pamphlet nor a broadsheet. Is a story.

GRACE: Religion has given us enough martyrs and saints. Is for us to do away with them, not create our own.

ROSE: Is not s'posed to be a list of facts and dates. There must be other women interested in recording exact history. I cannot do all. Is a story I have written, out of my imagination, to entertain. Not a bible.

GRACE: That leads me to other thing I want to say.

ROSE: Oh no, will mean I will have to start whole thing over.

GRACE: There is too many scenes of hanging and swimming and is not for us to present as entertainment.

ROSE: But that is the truth! One breath you say 'not accurate' the next you want women to sprout wings and fly out of the ponds. And next no doubt you'll tell me that the pricker's character is not light enough. Well, I care not. He is writ as he is. And what difference if he suffered from corn-toes or was kind to his dog. It does not lift weight off his wrongs.

GRACE: I have no quarrel with pricker's character. Though there will always be those who refuse to believe the worse has been done to us. But, Rose, do not give him all the weight. What of the fight back?

ROSE: But we've not stopped it. (*Then*:) I put bit about the bear in.

GRACE (*impatiently*): We? We've not stopped it? Look at you. What are you still doing in men's clothes?

ROSE: And how else am I to hold down job as shipping clerk and how else are we to be afforded protection. My clothes are of no matter. You don't like my play. Nothing matters.

GRACE: You will have to learn to take criticism with a little more dignity. Do you think they'll not be shouting at you from all sides?

Enter JANE.

JANE: I'm back. (*Sees* GRACE.) Christ Jesus, Grace, you look far from the best of health.

GRACE (*dryly*): Still got the same sweet, sensitive nature I perceive.

ROSE *rushes to* JANE *and hugs her,* JANE *lifting* ROSE *off the ground and swinging her round. Enter* URSULA, *her expression of agitation turns to confusion on seeing* ROSE *and* JANE. ROSE *wriggles out of* JANE's *grasp. An embarrassed silence ensues.*

JANE: I don't mind you have a new love, Rosie, but didn't you ever speak of me to her?

ROSE: Ursula is not my love as you term it.

JANE: Notice she's not jumped to a denial.

GRACE: She cannot hear Jane — she is deaf.

JANE (*casually*): Oh Aye?

(*Signs to* URSULA *and says:*) Is not Rose a wonderful woman?

URSULA (*signs*): Woman? Woman?

GRACE: Where on this earth did you learn to do that girl?

ROSE: The one time I thought your big mouth could go unheeded.

JANE: Just because I can't read and write, Grace, doesn't mean I can't converse in other ways.

(*To* ROSE:) You daft cony — is a wonder, your modesty's not brought bladder trouble on yourself.

URSULA (*signs to* JANE): If I'd known she could have come to the meeting by the pond.

JANE (*to* ROSE): If she'd known you could have come to the meeting.

ROSE: Oh we all been there before.

JANE (*to* ROSE): By the pond. (*Pause.*) Oh no, the man of hanging tree is yet alive and pricking.

ROSE (*agitated*): When? Who was swam? What was her name? Is she alive?

GRACE: Keep your clacker still, Rosie. Let Ursula tell us in her own way.

The others have made a model pricker by stuffing straw into a spare jerkin and a pair of breeches. They perform a 'dumb' show which URSULA *narrates in sign language. (It should be accompanied by a taped voice over.)*

URSULA (*with voice over*): We met the night before. Women from near and far and a very long and angry meeting it was; only one thing was agreed on by all — that we would meet in the morning and no woman that day would lose her life. So now we are stood at the pond. Our blood tingling and the pricker preening himself on drawing such a large crowd.

GRACE *stands the dummy pricker up and makes it take a bow.*

Everything still and I had half a thought of worry that we would take root in the ground. The feeling vanished when her body hit the water, we joined hands and by a force unspake floated through the crowd, each silent till she was set free.

The other three mime pulling the woman from the water.

ROSE (*to imaginary woman*): Take off there that wet cloth. Pass me those blankets. Who will take this woman home?

GRACE: I will, I be her sister.

JANE: And what shall we do for him?

ROSE: Smash his brain-pan and have done.

GRACE: Nay, we agreed not to do that. He must take his own medicine.

JANE: Cam on. Help me put this sheet over him.

They put the sheet over the struggling man.

GRACE: No, he must be prepared in same detail. Left thumb tied to right toe and right thumb tied to left toe.

JANE: Should be right thumb tied to left stone.

ROSE: I, for one, wouldn't be disappointed, if he were two stones lighter even if it did mean he did float.

They mime throwing him into the pond.

GRACE: Seems he has floated.

GRACE and JANE pull the dummy pricker up and drag him out of the action.

ROSE: And he is yet living.

JANE: Then who amongst us is agreed that he should complete the course of punishment?

URSULA (*voice over*): We did not kill him. We are not the same as him. We left him, still tied, in the place where women's bodies are left to be claimed by their loved ones at night.

End of show.

ROSE (*shouts*): Aye bodies. Bodies of dead women. Deemed then innocent for an invented crime. Dead to be collected and buried! How many of us will have to die while our good natures get the better of us?

Silence.

GRACE (*quietly*): Then take that pistol and shoot him through the head. For is that not what they do to sick animals? And tell him from me, t'is offer of death more humane than ever

he has dealt in.

It is JANE who turns with the purpose of doing so. ROSE remains, stunned by GRACE's change in attitude.

URSULA places her hand on JANE's arm to restrain her.

ROSE: Oh take heart, Jane, he has yet to escape his fate. He'll not get far tie tied and bound. Cold and dripping.

GRACE: Aye, then, so be it, let nature deal with him in her own way.

Scene Nine

The pond.
Night. The dummy has been replaced by the PRICKER, tied in the manner described and shivering uncontrollably. A WOMAN approaches.

MAN: Mother? Is that you?

She comes closer.

Oh, Mother, what has kept you so long?

MOTHER: The hardest hours of my life, far harder than the few before you were born.

MAN: Untie me, Mother. I shall perish of cold.

MOTHER: How many times have you done the same for me, son?

She turns.

MAN: Don't leave me.

MOTHER (*turns back*): And still you show no remorse.

MAN: Hurry. Please hurry, Mother.

MOTHER: Have you no word of shame?

MAN: Have I not had all day to think on my plight and shame enough, aye, to know I cannot live here. I will follow my brother to New England and make there a new life for myself.

MOTHER: And what of me?

MAN: You're to say I died of

consumption. You have access to parish register. Therein record my death.

MOTHER: And what of me?

MAN: You can't let me die. Mother, help me.

MOTHER: The cord which once bound us did not even enter your head whilst you hung many cords around my neck.

MAN: I vouchsafe I will n'ere show my face here again.

Pause.

MOTHER: You will not return?

MAN: Ne'er, untie me please.

MOTHER (*stooping to untie him*): I would that you had never been born, but I cannot take life from you.

URSULA (*voice over only*): We all knew what she'd done and that she aided his passage to Salem, but we never heard of him again and we never spoke of it again. We spoke to her, she was one of us.

Scene Ten

GRACE'*s garden.*
GRACE'*s burial.* HELEN *and* ROSE. LADY H, *obscured from their view, is digging the grave.*

HELEN: I know it is but small comfort, but Grace does now merit a grave within the churchyard.

ROSE: The comfort is she died peacefully. Was her own wish to be buried in her garden. And we'd best rouse ourselves, for one thing church'll not be lending us gravediggers.

HELEN: Oh Lady H is seeing to it.

ROSE: Lady H?!

HELEN: I tell you she is turning over a new leaf.

ROSE: She'll be turning over a site more than that.

They find LADY H *who has almost completed the work.*

LADY H (*wiping her muddy face with an equally muddy hand*): Will this do?

HELEN: Thank you very much, Lady H.

LADY H: H only from this day forth. For I am hoping to have proved myself a lady no longer.

ROSE: And thank you all the same. We are waiting now on Jane, and Ursula but I know not where she is.

LADY H: She'll be here presently for she wants to pay her own tribute to Grace. I will take my leave now, for I sense it is not my place to be here longer. (*Exits.*)

HELEN: Thank you.

A fussy little PARSON *bumbles breathlessly towards them.*

ROSE: Don't look now but God's little flea has cam to bug us. (*She walks towards him.*)

PARSON (*breathlessly*): You can't take burial services into your own hands. This place is unconsecrated ground. Do you want for her neighbours to . . .

ROSE (*firmly*): To say that she was a wise woman? An outlaw. Aye, I do.

PARSON: I forbid it, in the name of God the father, God the son . . .

ROSE: If God the Father and God the Son care to intervene on their own account that is up to them but on you own you'll not be able to sway us.

PARSON: You will bring nothing but an eternity of hell's fire and damnation on your head.

ROSE: That will be all? Then I'm laughing. (*She laughs. He exits. She returns to* HELEN.)

ROSE: Still they will not leave alone.

HELEN: Aye but Grace would've approved of manner in which you sent him off. She didn't want for today to be dreary.

ROSE (*sighs*): Aye she say's 'Rose is to take form of celebration' but is not an easy feeling to capture, Grace. Oh, Grace.

HELEN (*gently*): Why not see if Jane is far off. I will tend to what has to be done.

ROSE *walks until* HELEN *is out of view, and sits by a tree, head in her hands. Enter* JANE *carrying a metal box.*

JANE: Rosie?

ROSE (*looks up*): What kept you?

JANE: A dog collar with a person inside.

ROSE (*smiles*): I hope you made him no offer of aid.

JANE: Indeed I did, in form of my foot, but alas he didn't note it till he was on his face. That is enough talk of parsons. We are here to say farewell to Grace.

ROSE: Seems so final.

JANE: Supposing you'd never known her? Would you have known how to read? Or name the stars? Or tamed a bear? Or written a play? Or been as strong?

ROSE (*smiles*): So now is the time for supposing?

JANE: Is not her memory a part of our lives and are we not better for it?

ROSE: Aye.

They join HELEN *and* URSULA *for the ceremony.* URSULA *kneels throughout, and plants various herbs in the fresh earth.*

HELEN
ROSE   (*sing*):
JANE

The Burial Song

Death comes swiftly
life on earth
Is ended, ending
All together we are sending
One another to ourselves
Not forgotten, undertaking

To remember, not forget
Life does end but celebrating
One we knew and won't forget.

ROSE (*reads*):
With you I learnt the stars at night
We named the Bear, who gave a fright
At last I see that my disguise
Hid me from men who tell their lies
In bed and gaol and with their blades
Their war, their fear, their rape and
       raids
Our knowledge we have always shared
With our own sex for whom we cared
Men take from us the power to cure
By brutal means, they make a war
On what we held as our birthright
They cut us up, but we will fight
Not in their wars, dressed up as men,
Not by the pond when they say when,
But by the the very deed they fear,
Deny their power to leave us here:

Pause.

HELEN: Grace, your life occurred with the passing of women's healing to men's doctoring. Now their inventions continue without intervention. How many charms have we played with to guess at the sex of the unborn child? Their science will conquer the problem and what will become of our sex for there can be no place in the world where daughters are valued above sons as first-born child. We will miss you not only for your vision, Grace, but for your strength and it is in your memory we struggle to arrest the weapons from the masters' violent hands.

ROSE: Thank you Helen.

Silence.

HELEN: Rose, now I'm wanting to ask if you've had new thought on the school for midwives.

ROSE: How many times are we to buy back our birthright?

JANE: She'll not be swayed from teaching girls to read and write.

HELEN: Aye, that will be task enough.

JANE: Lady H has agreed to help us, but
Rose has to help her with her
education first. Her family have all
that money and they know nothing.

ROSE: You are welcome to join us,
Helen.

HELEN: Thank you but I shall carry on
with the Quakers.

JANE: Now, that do sound like a good
title for your next play, Rose.

HELEN: And what of your play? I hear
it is very good?

JANE: Aye and we should know, Ursula
and I have learned our writing by
copying it out — every word.

HELEN (*to* ROSE): So you will choose a
man's name?

ROSE: No. My own.

HELEN: No doubt I'll see it anon then.

JANE (*remembering*): That's why I
brought this box for copied version to
be secured within and buried next to
Grace.

ROSE: But it's not had a life yet.

HELEN: So if it doesn't cam to pass in
your lifetime one day when you're
long gone it'll be uncovered.

ROSE: But s'pose it never gets
unearthed?

JANE (*turning to face* ROSE): You're
not the only woman in the world,
Rose.

Further titles in the Methuen Modern Plays
and World Dramatists series are
described on the following pages.

Methuen's Modern Plays

Bertolt Brecht

Mother Courage and Her Children
The Caucasian Chalk Circle
The Good Person of Szechwan
The Life of Galileo
The Threepenny Opera
Saint Joan of the Stockyards
The Resistible Rise of Arturo Ui
The Mother
Mr Puntila and His Man Matti
The Measures Taken and other
    Lehrstücke
The Days of the Commune
The Messingkauf Dialogues
Man Equals Man and *The Elephant*
    Calf
The Rise and Fall of the City of
    Mahagonny and *The Seven Deadly Sins*
Baal
A Respectable Wedding and other one-act
    plays
Drums in the Night
In the Jungle of Cities
Fear and Misery of the Third Reich and
    Señora Carrar's Rifles
Schweyk in the Second World War and
    The Visions of Simone Machard

Brecht ⎫
Weill ⎬   *Happy End*
Lane ⎭

Howard Brenton

The Churchill Play
Weapons of Happiness
Epsom Downs
The Romans in Britain
Plays for the Poor Theatre
Magnificence
Revenge
Hitler Dances
Bloody Poetry

Howard Brenton and David Hare	*Brassneck*
	Pravda
Mikhail Bulgakov	*The White Guard*
Caryl Churchill	*Top Girls*
	Softcops and *Fen*
Noël Coward	*Hay Fever*
Sarah Daniels	*Masterpieces*
Shelagh Delaney	*A Taste of Honey*
	The Lion in Love
David Edgar	*Destiny*
	Mary Barnes
	Maydays
Michael Frayn	*Clouds*
	Make and Break
	Noises Off
	Benefactors
Max Frisch	*The Fire Raisers*
	Andorra
	Triptych
Simon Gray	*Butley*
	Otherwise Engaged and other plays
	Dog Days
	The Rear Column and other plays
	Close of Play and Pig in a Poke
	Stage Struck
	Quartermaine's Terms
	The Common Pursuit
Peter Handke	*Offending the Audience* and *Self-Accusation*
	Kaspar
	The Ride Across Lake Constance
	They Are Dying Out
Kaufman & Hart	*Once in a Lifetime, You Can't Take It With You* and *The Man Who Came To Dinner*
Vaclav Havel	*The Memorandum*

Barrie Keeffe	*Gimme Shelter (Gem, Gotcha, Getaway)*
	Barbarians (Killing Time, Abide With Me, In the City)
	A Mad World, My Masters
Arthur Kopit	*Indians*
	Wings
Larry Kramer	*The Normal Heart*
John McGrath	*The Cheviot, the Stag and the Black, Black Oil*
David Mamet	*Glengarry Glen Ross*
	American Buffalo
David Mercer	*After Haggerty*
	Cousin Vladimir and *Shooting the Chandelier*
	Duck Song
	The Monster of Karlovy Vary and *Then and Now*
	No Limits To Love
Arthur Miller	*The American Clock*
	The Archbishop's Ceiling
	Two-Way Mirror
	Danger: Memory!
Percy Mtwa	
Mbongeni Ngema	} *Woza Albert!*
Barney Simon	
Peter Nichols	*Passion Play*
	Poppy
Joe Orton	*Loot*
	What the Butler Saw
	Funeral Games and *The Good and Faithful Servant*
	Entertaining Mr Sloane
	Up Against It
Louise Page	*Golden Girls*
Harold Pinter	*The Birthday Party*
	The Room and *The Dumb Waiter*
	The Caretaker
	A Slight Ache and other plays
	The Collection and *The Lover*

	The Homecoming
	Tea Party and other plays
	Landscape and *Silence*
	Old Times
	No Man's Land
	Betrayal
	The Hothouse
	Other Places (*A Kind of Alaska, Victoria Station, Family Voices*)
Luigi Pirandello	*Henry IV*
	Six Characters in Search of an Author
Sephen Poliakoff	*Coming in to Land*
	Hitting Town and *City Sugar*
	Breaking the Silence
David Rudkin	*The Saxon Shore*
	The Sons of Light
	The Triumph of Death
Jean-Paul Sartre	*Crime Passionnel*
Wole Soyinka	*Madmen and Specialists*
	The Jero Plays
	Death and the King's Horseman
	A Play of Giants
C. P. Taylor	*And a Nighingale Sang . . .*
	Good
Peter Whelan	*The Accrington Pals*
Nigel Williams	*Line 'Em*
	Class Enemy
Theatre Workshop	*Oh What a Lovely War!*
Various authors	*Best Radio Plays of 1978* (Don Haworth: *Episode on a Thursday Evening;* Tom Mallin: *Halt! Who Goes There?;* Jennifer Phillips: *Daughters of Men;* Fay Weldon: *Polaris;* Jill Hyem: *Remember Me;* Richard Harris: *Is It Something I Said?*)
	Best Radio Plays of 1979 (Shirley Gee: *Typhoid Mary;* Carey Harrison: *I Never Killed My German;* Barrie Keeffe: *Heaven Scent;*

John Kirkmorris: *Coxcombe;* John
Peacock: *Attard in Retirement;* Olwen
Wymark: *The Child*)

Best Radio Plays of 1981 (Peter Barnes:
The Jumping Mimuses of Byzantium;
Don Haworth: *Talk of Love and War;*
Harold Pinter: *Family Voices;* David
Pownall: *Beef;* J P Rooney: *The Dead
Image;* Paul Thain: *The Biggest
Sandcastle in the World*)

Best Radio Plays of 1982 (Rhys
Adrian: *Watching the Plays Together;*
John Arden: *The Old Man Sleeps
Alone;* Harry Barton: *Hoopoe Day;*
Donald Chapman: *Invisible Writing;*
Tom Stoppard: *The Dog It Was
That Died;* William Trevor: *Autumn
Sunshine*)

Best Radio Plays of 1983 (Wally K Daly:
Time Slip; Shirley Gee: *Never in My
Lifetime;* Gerry Jones: *The Angels They
Grow Lonely;* Steve May: *No
Exceptions;* Martyn Read: *Scouting for
Boys*)

Best Radio Plays of 1984 (Stephen
Dunstone: *Who Is Sylvia?;* Don
Haworth: *Daybreak;* Robert Ferguson:
Transfigured Night; Caryl Phillips:
The Wasted Years; Christopher Russell:
Swimmer; Rose Tremain: *Temporary
Shelter*)

Best Radio Plays of 1985 (Rhys
Adrian: *Outpatient;* Barry
Collins: *King Canute;* Martin
Crimp: *The Attempted Acts;*
David Pownall: *Ploughboy
Monday;* James Saunders:
Menocchio; Michael Wall:
Hiroshima: The Movie)

World Dramatists

Collections of plays by the best-known modern playwrights in value-for-money paperbacks.

John Arden	PLAYS: ONE *Serjeant Musgrave's Dance, The Workhouse Donkey, Armstrong's Last Goodnight*
Brendan Behan	THE COMPLETE PLAYS *The Quare Fellow, The Hostage, Richard's Cork Leg, Moving Out, A Garden Party, The Big House*
Edward Bond	PLAYS: ONE *Saved, Early Morning, The Pope's Wedding* PLAYS: TWO *Lear, The Sea, Narrow Road to the Deep North, Black Mass, Passion*
Howard Brenton	PLAYS: ONE *Christie in Love, Magnificence, The Churchill Play, Weapons of Happiness, Epsom Downs, Sore Throats*
Georg Büchner	THE COMPLETE PLAYS *Danton's Death, Leonce and Lena, Woyzeck* with *The Hessian Courier, Lenz, On Cranial Nerves* and *Selected Letters*
Caryl Churchill	PLAYS: ONE *Owners, Traps, Vinegar Tom, Light Shining in Buckinghamshire, Cloud Nine*
Noël Coward	PLAYS: ONE *Hay Fever, The Vortex, Fallen Angels, Easy Virtue*

PLAYS: TWO
Private Lives, Bitter-Sweet, The
Marquise, Post-Mortem
PLAYS: THREE
Design for Living, Cavalcade,
Conversation Piece, To-night at 8.30
(*Hands Across the Sea, Still Life,*
Fumed Oak)
PLAYS: FOUR
Blithe Spirit, Present Laughter, This
Happy Breed, To-night at 8.30 (*Ways*
and Means, The Astonished Heart,
'Red Peppers')
PLAYS: FIVE
Relative Values, Look After Lulu!,
Waiting in the Wings, Suite in Three
Keys

David Edgar
PLAYS: ONE
Destiny, Mary Barnes, The Jail Diary
of Albie Sachs, Saigon Rose, O Fair
Jerusalem

Michael Frayn
PLAYS: ONE
Alphabetical Order, Donkey's Years,
Clouds, Make and Break, Noises Off

John Galsworthy
FIVE PLAYS
Strife, Justice, The Eldest Son, The
Skin Game, Loyalties

Simon Gray
PLAYS: ONE
Butley, Otherwise Engaged, The Rear
Column, Quartermaine's Terms, The
Common Pursuit

Henrik Ibsen
PLAYS: ONE
Ghosts, The Wild Duck, The Master
Builder
PLAYS: TWO
A Doll's House, An Enemy of the
People, Hedda Gabler

PLAYS: THREE
*The Homecoming, Tea Party, The
Basement, Landscape, Silence, That's
Your Trouble, That's All, Applicant,
Interview, Dialogue for Three, Night*
PLAYS: FOUR
*Old Times, No Man's Land, Betrayal,
Monologue, Family Voices*

Luigi Pirandello   THREE PLAYS
*The Rules of the Game, Six
Characters in Search of an Author,
Henry IV*

Terence Rattigan   PLAYS: ONE
*French Without Tears, The Winslow
Boy, The Browning Version,
Harlequinade*
PLAYS: TWO
*The Deep Blue Sea, Separate Tables,
In Praise of Love, Before Dawn*

Sophocles   THE THEBAN PLAYS
*Oedipus the King, Oedipus at Colonus,
Antigone*

August Strindberg   PLAYS: ONE
The Father, Miss Julie and *The Ghost
Sonata*
PLAYS: TWO
*A Dream Play, The Dance of Death,
The Stronger*

Wilde   THREE PLAYS
*The Importance of Being Earnest,
Lady Windermere's Fan, An Ideal
Husband*

Synge

THE COMPLETE PLAYS
*The Playboy of the Western World,
The Tinker's Wedding, In the Shadow
of the Glen, Riders to the Sea, The
Well of the Saints, Deirdre of the
Sorrows*